Confessions of a Sinner

St Augustine
AD 354–430

St Augustine

Confessions of a Sinner

TRANSLATED BY R. S. PINE-COFFIN

PENGUIN BOOKS — GREAT IDEAS

PENGUIN BOOKS

Published by the Penguin Group
Penguin Books Ltd, 80 Strand, London WC2R ORL, England
Penguin Group (USA) Inc., 375 Hudson Street, New York, New York 10014, USA
Penguin Books Australia Ltd, 250 Camberwell Road,
Camberwell, Victoria 3124, Australia
Penguin Books Canada Ltd, 10 Alcorn Avenue, Toronto, Ontario, Canada M4V 3B2
Penguin Books India (P) Ltd, 11 Community Centre,
Panchsheel Park, New Delhi – 110 017, India
Penguin Group (NZ), Cnr Airborne and Rosedale Roads,
Albany, Auckland 1310, New Zealand
Penguin Books (South Africa) (Pty) Ltd, 24 Sturdee Avenue,
Rosebank 2196, South Africa

Penguin Books Ltd, Registered Offices: 80 Strand, London WC2R ORL, England

www.penguin.com

Confessions first published in Penguin Classics 1961
This extract first published in Penguin Books 2004

023

Translation copyright © R. S. Pine-Coffin, 1961
All rights reserved

Taken from the Penguin Classics edition *Confessions*,
translated by R. S. Pine-Coffin

Set in Monotype Dante
Typeset by Rowland Phototypesetting Ltd, Bury St Edmunds, Suffolk
Printed and bound in Great Britain by Clays Ltd, Elcograf S.p.A.

ISBN-13: 978-0-141-01883-6
ISBN-10: 0-141-01883-6

www.greenpenguin.co.uk

Penguin Books is committed to a sustainable
future for our business, our readers and our planet.
This book is made from Forest Stewardship
Council™ certified paper.

Contents

Book I

1

*Can any praise be worthy of the Lord's majesty? How magnifi-
cent his strength! How inscrutable his wisdom!* Man is one
of your creatures, Lord, and his instinct is to praise you.
He bears about him the mark of death, the sign of his
own sin, to remind him that you *thwart the proud.* But
still, since he is a part of your creation, he wishes to
praise you. The thought of you stirs him so deeply that
he cannot be content unless he praises you, because you
made us for yourself and our hearts find no peace until
they rest in you.

[. . .]

Those who look for the Lord will cry out in praise of him,
because all who look for him shall find him, and when
they find him they will praise him. I shall look for you,
Lord, by praying to you and as I pray I shall believe in
you, because we have had preachers to tell us about you.
It is my faith that calls to you, Lord, the faith which you
gave me and made to live in me through the merits of
your Son, who became man, and through the ministry
of your preacher.

6

But, dust and ashes though I am, let me appeal to your pity, since it is to you in your mercy that I speak, not to a man, who would simply laugh at me. Perhaps you too may laugh at me, but you will relent and have pity on me. For all I want to tell you, Lord, is that I do not know where I came from when I was born into this life which leads to death – or should I say, this death which leads to life? This much is hidden from me. But, although I do not remember it all myself, I know that when I came into the world all the comforts which your mercy provides were there ready for me. This I was told by my parents, the father who begat me and the mother who conceived me, the two from whose bodies you formed me in the limits of time. So it was that I was given the comfort of woman's milk.

[. . .]

I do acknowledge you, Lord of heaven and earth, and I praise you for my first beginnings, although I cannot remember them. But you have allowed men to discover these things about themselves by watching other babies, and also to learn much from what women have to tell. I know that I was a living person even at that age, and as I came towards the end of infancy I tried to find signs to convey my feelings to others. Where could such a living creature come from if not from you, O Lord? Can it be that any man has skill to fabricate himself? Or can there be some channel by which we derive our life and our very existence from some other source than you? Surely we can only derive them from our Maker, from you, Lord, to whom living and being are not different things, since infinite life and infinite being are one and the same. For you are infinite and never change. In you 'today' never comes to an end: and yet our 'today' does come to an end in you, because time, as well as everything else, exists in you. If it did not, it would have no means of passing. And since your years never come to an end, for you they are simply 'today'. The countless days of our lives and of our forefathers' lives have passed by within your 'today'. From it they have received their due measure of duration and their very existence. And so it will be with all the other days which are still to come. But you yourself are eternally the same. In your 'today' you will make all that is to exist tomorrow and thereafter, and in your 'today' you have made all that existed yesterday and for ever before.

Need it concern me if some people cannot understand this? Let them ask what it means, and be glad to ask: but they may content themselves with the question alone. For it is better for them to find you and leave the question unanswered than to find the answer without finding you.

7

Hear me, O God! How wicked are the sins of men! Men say this and you pity them, because you made man, but you did not make sin in him.

Who can recall to me the sins I committed as a baby? For in your sight no man is free from sin, not even a child who has lived only one day on earth. Who can show me what my sins were? Some small baby in whom I can see all that I do not remember about myself? What sins, then, did I commit when I was a baby myself? Was it a sin to cry when I wanted to feed at the breast? I am too old now to feed on mother's milk, but if I were to cry for the kind of food suited to my age, others would rightly laugh me to scorn and remonstrate with me. So then too I deserved a scolding for what I did; but since I could not have understood the scolding, it would have been unreasonable, and most unusual, to rebuke me. We root out these faults and discard them as we grow up, and this is proof enough that they are faults, because I have never seen a man purposely throw out the good when he clears away the bad. It can hardly be right for a child, even at that age, to cry for everything, including things which would harm him; to work himself into a tantrum against people older than himself and not required to obey him; and to try his best to strike and hurt others who know better than he does, including his own parents, when they do not give in to him and refuse to pander to whims which would only do him harm.

4

This shows that, if babies are innocent, it is not for lack of will to do harm, but for lack of strength.

[. . .]

I do not remember that early part of my life, O Lord, but I believe what other people have told me about it and from watching other babies I can conclude that I also lived as they do. But, true though my conclusions may be, I do not like to think of that period as part of the same life I now lead, because it is dim and forgotten and, in this sense, it is no different from the time I spent in my mother's womb. But if *I was born in sin and guilt was with me already when my mother conceived me*, where, I ask you, Lord, where or when was I, your servant, ever innocent? But I will say no more about that time, for since no trace of it remains in my memory, it need no longer concern me.

9

But, O God my God, I now went through a period of suffering and humiliation. I was told that it was right and proper for me as a boy to pay attention to my teachers, so that I should do well at my study of grammar and get on in the world. This was the way to gain the respect of others and win for myself what passes for wealth in this world. So I was sent to school to learn to read. I was too small to understand what purpose it might serve and yet, if I was idle at my studies, I was beaten for it, because beating was favoured by tradition. Countless boys long since forgotten had built up this stony path for us to tread and we were made to pass along it, adding to the toil and sorrow of the sons of Adam.

But we found that some men prayed to you, Lord, and we learned from them to do the same, thinking of you in the only way that we could understand, as some great person who could listen to us and help us, even though we could not see you or hear you or touch you. I was still a boy when I first began to pray to you, my Help and Refuge. I used to prattle away to you, and though I was small, my devotion was great when I begged you not to let me be beaten at school. Sometimes, for my own good, you did not grant my prayer, and then my elders and even my parents, who certainly wished me no harm, would laugh at the beating I got – and in those days beatings were my one great bugbear.

[. . .]

11

While still a boy I had been told of the eternal life promised to us by Our Lord, who humbled himself and came down amongst us proud sinners. As a catechumen, I was blessed regularly from birth with the sign of the Cross and was seasoned with God's salt, for, O Lord, my mother placed great hope in you. Once as a child I was taken suddenly ill with a disorder of the stomach and was on the point of death. You, my God, were my guardian even then, and you saw the fervour and strength of my faith as I appealed to the piety of my own mother and to the mother of us all, your Church, to give me the baptism of Christ your Son, who is my God and my Master. My earthly mother was deeply anxious, because in the pure faith of her heart, she was in greater labour to ensure my eternal salvation than she had been at my birth. Had I not quickly recovered, she would have hastened to see that I was admitted to the sacraments of salvation and washed clean by acknowledging you, Lord Jesus, for the pardon of my sins. So my washing in the waters of baptism was postponed, in the surmise that, if I continued to live, I should defile myself again with sin and, after baptism, the guilt of pollution would be greater and more dangerous. Even at that age I already believed in you, and so did my mother and the whole household except for my father. But, in my heart, he did not gain the better of my mother's piety and prevent me from believing in Christ just because he still disbelieved himself. For she did all that she could to see that you, my God, should be a Father to me rather than he. In this you helped her to turn the scales against her husband, whom she always obeyed because by obeying him she obeyed your law, thereby showing greater virtue than he did.

I ask you, my God – for, if it is your will, I long to know – for what purpose was my baptism postponed at that time? Was it for my good that the reins which held me from sin were slackened? Or is it untrue that they were slackened? If not, why do we continually hear people say, even nowadays, 'Leave him alone and let him do it. He is not yet baptized'? Yet when the health of the body is at stake, no one says 'Let him get worse. He is not yet cured.' It would, then, have been much better if I had been healed at once and if all that I and my family could do had been done to make sure that once my sould had received its salvation, its safety should be left in your keeping, since its salvation had come from you. This would surely have been the better course. But my mother well knew how many great tides of temptation threatened me before I grew up, and she chose to let them beat upon the as yet unmoulded clay rather than upon the finished image which had received the stamp of baptism.

17

Let me tell you, my God, how I squandered the brains you gave me on foolish delusions. I was set a task which troubled me greatly, for if I were successful, I might win some praise: if not, I was afraid of disgrace or a beating. I had to recite the speech of Juno, who was pained and angry because she could not prevent Aeneas from sailing to Italy. I had been told that Juno had never really spoken the words, but we were compelled to make believe and follow the flight of the poet's fancy by repeating in prose what he had said in verse. The contest was to be won by the boy who found the best words to suit the meaning and best expressed feelings of sorrow and anger appropriate to the majesty of the character he impersonated.

What did all this matter to me, my God, my true Life? Why did my recitation win more praise than those of the many other boys in my class? Surely it was all so much smoke without fire? Was there no other subject on which I might have sharpened my wits and my tongue? I might have used them, O Lord, to praise you in the words of your Scriptures, which could have been a prop to support my heart, as if it were a young vine, so that it would not have produced this crop of worthless fruit, fit only for the birds to peck at. For offerings can be made to those birds of prey, the fallen angels, in more ways than one.

19

It was at the threshold of a world such as this that I stood in peril as a boy. I was already being prepared for its tournaments by a training which taught me to have a horror of faulty grammar instead of teaching me, when I committed these faults, not to envy others who avoided them. All this, my God, I admit and confess to you. By these means I won praise from the people whose favour I sought, for I thought that the right way to live was to do as they wished. I was blind to the whirlpool of debasement in which I had been plunged away from the sight of your eyes. For in your eyes nothing could be more debased than I was then, since I was even troublesome to the people whom I set out to please. Many and many a time I lied to my tutor, my masters, and my parents, and deceived them because I wanted to play

games or watch some futile show or was impatient to
imitate what I saw on the stage. I even stole from my
parents' larder and from their table, either from greed
or to get something to give to other boys in exchange
for their favourite toys, which they were willing to barter
with me. And in the games I played with them I often
cheated in order to come off the better, simply because
a vain desire to win had got the better of me. And yet
there was nothing I could less easily endure, nothing
that made me quarrel more bitterly, than to find others
cheating me as I cheated them. All the same, if they
found me out and blamed me for it, I would lose my
temper rather than give in.

Can this be the innocence of childhood? Far from it,
O Lord! But I beg you to forgive it. For commanders
and kings may take the place of tutors and schoolmasters,
nuts and balls and pet birds may give way to money and
estates and servants, but these same passions remain
with us while one stage of life follows upon another, just
as more severe punishments follow upon the school-
master's cane. It was, then, simply because they are small
that you used children to symbolize humility when, as
our King, you commended it by saying that *the kingdom
of heaven belongs to such as these.*

20

And yet, Lord, even if you had willed that I should not
survive my childhood, I should have owed you gratitude,
because you are our God, the supreme Good, the Creator

and Ruler of the universe. For even as a child I existed, I was alive, I had the power of feeling; I had an instinct to keep myself safe and sound, to preserve my own being, which was a trace of the single unseen Being from whom it was derived; I had an inner sense which watched over my bodily senses and kept them in full vigour; and even in the small things which occupied my thoughts I found pleasure in the truth. I disliked finding myself in the wrong; my memory was good; I was acquiring the command of words; I enjoyed the company of friends; and I shrank from pain, ignorance, and sorrow. Should I not be grateful that so small a creature possessed such wonderful qualities? But they were all gifts from God, for I did not give them to myself. His gifts are good and the sum of them all is my own self. Therefore, the God who made me must be good and all the good in me is his. I thank him and praise him for all the good in my life, even my life as a boy. But my sin was this, that I looked for pleasure, beauty, and truth not in him but in myself and his other creatures, and the search led me instead to pain, confusion, and error. My God, in whom is my delight, my glory, and my trust, I thank you for your gifts and beg you to preserve and keep them for me. Keep me, too, and so your gifts will grow and reach perfection and I shall be with you myself, for I should not even exist if it were not by your gift.

Book II

I must now carry my thoughts back to the abominable things I did in those days, the sins of the flesh which defiled my soul. I do this, my God, not because I love those sins, but so that I may love you. For love of your love I shall retrace my wicked ways. The memory is bitter, but it will help me to savour your sweetness, the sweetness that does not deceive but brings real joy and never fails. For love of your love I shall retrieve myself from the havoc of disruption which tore me to pieces when I turned away from you, whom alone I should have sought, and lost myself instead on many a different quest. For as I grew to manhood I was inflamed with desire for a surfeit of hell's pleasures. Foolhardy as I was, I ran wild with lust that was manifold and rank. In your eyes my beauty vanished and I was foul to the core, yet I was pleased with my own condition and anxious to be pleasing in the eyes of men.

2

I cared for nothing but to love and be loved. But my love went beyond the affection of one mind for another, beyond the arc of the bright beam of friendship. Bodily desire, like a morass, and adolescent sex welling up within me exuded mists which clouded over and obscured my heart, so that I could not distinguish the clear light of true love from the murk of lust. Love and lust together seethed within me. In my tender youth they swept me away over the precipice of my body's appetites and plunged me in the whirlpool of sin. More and more I angered you, unawares. For I had been deafened by the clank of my chains, the fetters of the death which was my due to punish the pride in my soul. I strayed still farther from you and you did not restrain me. I was tossed and spilled, floundering in the broiling sea of my fornication, and you said no word. How long it was before I learned that you were my true joy! You were silent then, and I went on my way, farther and farther from you, proud in my distress and restless in fatigue, sowing more and more seeds whose only crop was grief.

[. . .]

3

In the same year my studies were interrupted. I had already begun to go to the near-by town of Madaura to study literature and the art of public speaking, but I was brought back home while my father, a modest citizen of Thagaste whose determination was greater than his means, saved up the money to send me farther afield to Carthage. I need not tell all this to you, my God, but in your presence I tell it to my own kind, to those other men, however few, who may perhaps pick up this book. And I tell it so that I and all who read my words may realize the depths from which we are to cry to you. Your ears will surely listen to the cry of a penitent heart which lives the life of faith.

[. . .]

4

It is certain, O Lord, that theft is punished by your law, the law that is written in men's hearts and cannot be erased however sinful they are. For no thief can bear that another thief should steal from him, even if he is rich and the other is driven to it by want. Yet I was willing to steal, and steal I did, although I was not compelled by any lack, unless it were the lack of a sense of justice or a distaste for what was right and a greedy love of doing wrong. For of what I stole I already had plenty, and much better at that, and I had no wish to enjoy the things I coveted by stealing, but only to enjoy the theft itself and the sin. There was a pear-tree near our vineyard, loaded with fruit that was attractive neither to look at nor to taste. Late one night a band of ruffians, myself included, went off to shake down the fruit and carry it away, for we had continued our games out of doors until well after dark, as was our pernicious habit. We took away an enormous quantity of pears, not to eat them ourselves, but simply to throw them to the pigs. Perhaps we ate some of them, but our real pleasure consisted in doing something that was forbidden.

[. . .]

6

If the crime of theft which I committed that night as a boy of sixteen were a living thing, I could speak to it and ask what it was that, to my shame, I loved in it. I had no beauty because it was a robbery. It is true that the pears which we stole had beauty, because they were created by you, the good God, who are the most beautiful of all beings and the Creator of all things, the supreme Good and my own true Good. But it was not the pears that my unhappy soul desired. I had plenty of my own, better than those, and I only picked them so that I might steal. For no sooner had I picked them than I threw them away, and tasted nothing in them but my own sin, which

I relished and enjoyed. If any part of one of those pears passed my lips, it was the sin that gave it flavour.

[. . .]

What was it, then, that pleased me in that act of theft? Which of my Lord's powers did I imitate in a perverse and wicked way? Since I had no real power to break his law, was it that I enjoyed at least the pretence of doing so, like a prisoner who creates for himself the illusion of liberty by doing something wrong, when he has no fear of punishment, under a feeble hallucination of power? Here was the slave who ran away from his master and chased a shadow instead! What an abomination! What a parody of life! What abysmal death! Could I enjoy doing wrong for no other reason than that it was wrong?

Book III

1

I went to Carthage, where I found myself in the midst of a hissing cauldron of lust. I had not yet fallen in love, but I was in love with the idea of it, and this feeling that something was missing made me despise myself for not being more anxious to satisfy the need. I began to look around for some object for my love, since I badly wanted to love something. I had no liking for the safe path without pitfalls, for although my real need was for you, my God, who are the food of the soul, I was not aware of this hunger. I felt no need for the food that does not perish, not because I had had my fill of it, but because the more I was starved of it the less palatable it seemed. Because of this my soul fell sick. It broke out in ulcers and looked about desperately for some material, worldly means of relieving the itch which they caused. But material things, which have no soul, could not be true objects for my love. To love and to have my love returned was my heart's desire, and it would be all the sweeter if I could also enjoy the body of the one who loved me.

[. . .]

3

Yet all the while, far above, your mercy hovered faith-
fully about me. I exhausted myself in depravity, in the
pursuit of an unholy curiosity. I deserted you and sank
to the bottom-most depths of scepticism and the mockery of devil-worship. My sins were a sacrifice to the devil,
and for all of them you chastised me. I defied you even
so far as to relish the thought of lust, and gratify it too,
within the walls of your church during the celebration
of your mysteries. For such a deed I deserved to pluck
the fruit of death, and you punished me for it with a
heavy lash. But, compared with my guilt, the penalty
was nothing. How infinite is your mercy, my God! You
are my Refuge from the terrible dangers amongst which
I wandered, head on high, intent upon withdrawing still
further from you. I loved my own way, not yours, but
it was a truant's freedom that I loved.

Besides these pursuits I was also studying for the
law. Such ambition was held to be honourable and I
determined to succeed in it. The more unscrupulous I
was, the greater my reputation was likely to be, for men
are so blind that they even take pride in their blindness.
By now I was at the top of the school of rhetoric. I
was pleased with my superior status and swollen with
conceit. All the same, as you well know, Lord, I behaved
far more quietly than the 'Wreckers', a title of ferocious
devilry which the fashionable set chose for themselves.
I had nothing whatever to do with their outbursts of
violence, but I lived amongst them, feeling a perverse

sense of shame because I was not like them. I kept company with them and there were times when I found their friendship a pleasure, but I always had a horror of what they did when they lived up to their name. Without provocation they would set upon some timid newcomer, gratuitously affronting his sense of decency for their own amusement and using it as fodder for their spiteful jests. This was the devil's own behaviour or not far different. 'Wreckers' was a fit name for them, for they were already adrift and total wrecks themselves. The mockery and trickery which they loved to practise on others was a secret snare of the devil, by which they were mocked and tricked themselves.

4

These were the companions with whom I studied the art of eloquence at that impressionable age. It was my ambition to be a good speaker, for the unhallowed and inane purpose of gratifying human vanity. The prescribed course of study brought me to a work by an author named Cicero, whose writing nearly everyone admires, if not the spirit of it. The title of the book is *Hortensius* and it recommends the reader to study philosophy. It altered my outlook on life. It changed my prayers to you, O Lord, and provided me with new hopes and aspirations. All my empty dreams suddenly lost their charm and my heart began to throb with a bewildering passion for the wisdom of eternal truth. I began to climb out of the depths to which I had sunk, in order to return to you. For I did not use the book as a whetstone to sharpen my tongue. It was not the style of it but the contents which won me over, and yet the allowance which my mother paid me was supposed to be spent on putting an edge on my tongue. I was now in my nineteenth year and she supported me, because my father had died two years before.

[...]

But, O Light of my heart, you know that at that time, although Paul's words were not known to me, the only thing that pleased me in Cicero's book was his advice not simply to admire one or another of the schools of philosophy, but to love wisdom itself, whatever it might be, and to search for it, pursue it, hold it, and embrace it firmly. These were the words which excited me and set me burning with fire, and the only check to this blaze of enthusiasm was that they made no mention of the name of Christ. For by your mercy, Lord, from the time when my mother fed me at the breast my infant heart had been suckled dutifully on his name, the name of your Son, my Saviour. Deep inside my heart his name remained, and nothing could entirely captivate me, however learned, however neatly expressed, however true it might be, unless his name were in it.

5

So I made up my mind to examine the holy Scriptures
and see what kind of books they were. I discovered
something that was at once beyond the understanding
of the proud and hidden from the eyes of children. Its
gait was humble, but the heights it reached were sublime.
It was enfolded in mysteries, and I was not the kind of
man to enter into it or bow my head to follow where it
led. But these were not the feelings I had when I first
read the Scriptures. To me they seemed quite unworthy
of comparison with the stately prose of Cicero, because
I had too much conceit to accept their simplicity and not
enough insight to penetrate their depths. It is surely true
that as the child grows these books grow with him. But
I was too proud to call myself a child. I was inflated with
self-esteem, which made me think myself a great man.

11

But *you sent down your help from above* and rescued my
soul from the depths of this darkness because my mother,
your faithful servant, wept to you for me, shedding more
tears for my spiritual death than other mothers shed for
the bodily death of a son. For in her faith and in the spirit
which she had from you she looked on me as dead. You
heard her and did not despise the tears which streamed
down and watered the earth in every place where she
bowed her head in prayer. You heard her, for how else

can I explain the dream with which you consoled her, so that she agreed to live with me and eat at the same table in our home? Lately she had refused to do this, because she loathed and shunned the blasphemy of my false beliefs.

She dreamed that she was standing on a wooden rule, and coming towards her in a halo of splendour she saw a young man who smiled at her in joy, although she herself was sad and quite consumed with grief. He asked her the reason for her sorrow and her daily tears, not because he did not know, but because he had something to tell her, for this is what happens in visions. When she replied that her tears were for the soul I had lost, he told her to take heart for, if she looked carefully, she would see that where she was, there also was I. And when she looked, she saw me standing beside her on the same rule.

Where could this dream have come from, unless it was that you listened to the prayer of her heart? For your goodness is almighty; you take good care of each of us as if you had no others in your care, and you look after all as you look after each. And surely it was for the same reason that, when she told me of the dream and I tried to interpret it as a message that she need not despair of being one day such as I was then, she said at once and without hesitation 'No! He did not say "Where he is, you are", but "Where you are, he is".'

[. . .]

12

I remember that in the meantime you gave her another answer to her prayers, though there is much besides this that escapes my memory and much too that I must omit, because I am in haste to pass on to other things, which I am more anxious to confess to you.

This other answer you gave her through the mouth of one of your priests, a bishop who had lived his life in the Church and was well versed in the Scriptures. My mother asked him, as a favour, to have a talk with me, so that he might refute my errors, drive the evil out of my mind, and replace it with good. He often did this when he found suitable pupils, but he refused to do it for me – a wise decision, as I afterwards realized. He told her that I was still unripe for instruction because, as she had told him, I was brimming over with the novelty of the heresy and had already upset a great many simple people with my casuistry. 'Leave him alone', he said. 'Just pray to God for him. From his own reading he will discover his mistakes and the depth of his profanity.'

At the same time he told her that when he was a child his misguided mother had handed him over to the Manichees. He had not only read almost all their books, but had also made copies of them, and even though no one argued the case with him or put him right, he had seen for himself that he ought to have nothing to do with the sect; and accordingly he had left it. Even after she had heard this my mother still would not be pacified, but persisted all the more with her tears and her entreaties that he should see me and discuss the matter. At last he grew impatient and said 'Leave me and go in peace. It cannot be that the son of these tears should be lost.'

In later years, as we talked together, she used to say that she accepted these words as a message from heaven.

Book IV

During the space of those nine years, from the nineteenth to the twenty-eighth year of my life, I was led astray myself and led others astray in my turn. We were alike deceivers and deceived in all our different aims and ambitions, both publicly when we expounded our so-called liberal ideas, and in private through our service to what we called religion. In public we were cocksure, in private superstitious, and everywhere void and empty. On the one hand we would hunt for worthless popular distinctions, the applause of an audience, prizes for poetry, or quickly fading wreaths won in competition. We loved the idle pastimes of the stage and in self-indulgence we were unrestrained. On the other hand we aspired to be purged of these lowly pleasures by taking food to the holy elect, as they were called, so that in their paunches it might pass through the process of being made into angels and gods who would set us free. These were the objects I pursued and the tasks I performed together with friends who, like myself and through my fault, were under the same delusion.

[. . .]

2

During those years I was a teacher of the art of public speaking. Love of money had gained the better of me and for it I sold to others the means of coming off the better in debate. But you know, Lord, that I preferred to have honest pupils, in so far as honesty has any meaning nowadays, and I had no evil intent when I taught the tricks of pleading, for I never meant them to be used to get the innocent condemned but, if the occasion arose, to save the lives of the guilty. From a distance, my God, you saw me losing my foothold on this treacherous ground, but through clouds of smoke you also saw a spark of good faith in me; for though, as I schooled my pupils, I was merely abetting their futile designs and their schemes of duplicity, nevertheless I did my best to teach them honestly.

In those days I lived with a woman, not my lawful wedded wife but a mistress whom I had chosen for no special reason but that my restless passions had alighted on her. But she was the only one and I was faithful to her. Living with her I found out by my own experience the difference between the restraint of the marriage alliance, contracted for the purpose of having children, and a bargain struck for lust, in which the birth of children is begrudged, though, if they come, we cannot help but love them.

[. . .]

12

If the things of this world delight you, praise God for them but turn your love away from them and give it to their Maker, so that in the things that please you you may not displease him. If your delight is in souls, love them in God, because they too are frail and stand firm only when they cling to him. If they do not, they go their own way and are lost. Love them, then, in him and draw as many with you to him as you can. Tell them 'He is the one we should love. He made the world and he stays close to it.' For when he made the world he did not go away and leave it. By him it was created and in him it exists. Wherever we taste the truth, God is there. He is in our very inmost hearts, but our hearts have strayed from him. *Think well on it, unbelieving hearts* and cling to him who made you. Stand with him and you shall not fall; rest in him and peace shall be yours. What snags and pitfalls lie before you? Where do your steps lead you? The good things which you love are all from God, but they are good and sweet only as long as they are used to do his will. They will rightly turn bitter if God is spurned and the things that come from him are wrongly loved. Why do you still choose to travel by this hard and arduous path? There is no rest to be found where you seek it. In the land of death you try to find a happy life: it is not there. How can life be happy where there is no life at all?

Our Life himself came down into this world and took away our death. He slew it with his own abounding life, and with thunder in his voice he called us from this world to return to him in heaven. From heaven he came down to us, entering first the Virgin's womb, where humanity, our mortal flesh, was wedded to him so that it might not be for ever mortal. Then *as a bridegroom coming from his bed, he exulted like some great runner who sees the track before him.* He did not linger on his way but ran, calling us to return to him, calling us by his words and deeds, by his life and death, by his descent into hell and his ascension into heaven. He departed from our sight, so that we should turn to our hearts and find him there. He departed, but he is here with us. He would not stay long with us, but he did not leave us. He went back to the place which he had never left, because *he, through whom the world was made, was in the world* and he *came into the world to save sinners.* To him my soul confesses and he is its Healer, because the wrong it did was against him. *Great ones of the world, will your hearts always be hardened?* Your Life has come down from heaven: will you not now at last rise with him and live? But how can you rise if you are in high places and your *clamour reaches heaven?* Come down from those heights, for then you may climb and, this time, climb to God. To climb against him was your fall.

[. . .]

13

I did not know this then. I was in love with beauty of a lower order and it was dragging me down. I used to ask my friends 'Do we love anything unless it is beautiful? What, then, is beauty and in what does it consist? What is it that attracts us and wins us over to the things we love? Unless there were beauty and grace in them, they would be powerless to win our hearts.' When I looked at things, it struck me that there was a difference between the beauty of an object considered by itself as one whole and the beauty to be found in a proper proportion between separate things, such as the due balance between the whole of the body and any of its limbs, or between the foot and the shoe with which it is shod, and so on. This idea burst from my heart like water from a spring. My mind was full of it and I wrote a book called *Beauty and Proportion*, in two or three volumes as far as I remember. You know how many there were, O Lord. I have forgotten, because by some chance the book was lost and I no longer have it.

14

O Lord, my God, what induced me to dedicate my book to Hierius, the great public speaker at Rome? I had never even seen him, but I admired his brilliant reputation for learning and had been greatly struck by what I had heard of his speeches. Even more than this I was impressed by the admiration which other people had for him. They overwhelmed him with praise, because it seemed extraordinary that a man born in Syria and originally trained to speak in Greek had later become so remarkable a speaker in Latin, and had also such a wealth of knowledge of the subjects studied by philosophers.

We can admire persons whom we have never seen, if we hear them praised, though this does not mean that simply to hear their praises will make us admire them. But enthusiasm in one man will kindle the same fire in another, for we admire the person whose praises we hear only if we believe that they are sincerely uttered – in other words that the person who utters them genuinely admires the man whom he praises.

[. . .]

But Hierius was the kind of man in whom I admired qualities that I would have been glad to possess. In my pride I was running adrift, at the mercy of every wind. You were guiding me as a helmsman steers a ship, but the course you steered was beyond my understanding. I know now, and confess it as the truth, that I admired Hierius more because others praised him than for the accomplishments for which they praised him. I know this because those same people, instead of praising him, might have abused him. They might have spoken of the same talents in him but found fault with them and despised them. If they had done this, my feelings would not have been aroused nor my admiration kindled. Yet his qualities would have been the same and he himself would have been no different. The only difference would have been in their attitude towards him.

We can see from this that the soul is weak and helpless unless it clings to the firm rock of truth. Men give voice to their opinions, but they are only opinions, like so many puffs of wind that waft the soul hither and thither and make it veer and turn. The light is clouded over and the truth cannot be seen, although it is there before our eyes. I thought it a matter of much importance to myself to bring my book and the work I had done to the notice of this great man. If he had approved of them, my fervour would have been all the more ardent. If he had found fault, my heart, which was empty and bereft of God's firm truth, would have suffered a cruel blow. Yet I found pleasure in giving my mind to the problem of beauty and proportion, the work which I had dedicated to him. Although I found no others to admire it, I was proud of it myself.

15

[. . .]

I was struggling to reach you, but you thrust me back so that I knew the taste of death. For *you thwart the proud*. And what greater pride could there be than to assert, as I did in my strange madness, that by nature I was what you are? I was changeable, and I knew it; for if I wanted to be a learned man, it could only mean that I wanted to be better than I was. All the same I preferred to think that you too were changeable rather than suppose that I was not what you are. This was why you thrust me back and crushed my rearing pride, while my imagination continued to play on material forms. Myself a man of flesh and blood I blamed the flesh. I was as fickle as *a breath of wind*, unable to return to you. I drifted on, making my way towards things that had no existence in you or in myself or in the body. They were not created for me by your truth but were the inventions of my own foolish imagination working on material things. Though I did not know it, I was in exile from my place in God's city among his faithful children, my fellow citizens. But I was all words, and stupidly I used to ask them, 'If, as you say, God made the soul, why does it err?' Yet I did not like them to ask me in return, 'If what you say is true, why does God err?' So I used to argue that your unchangeable substance, my God, was forced to err, rather than admit that my own was changeable and erred of its own free will, and that its errors were my punishment.

[. . .]

16

When I was only about twenty years of age Aristotle's book on the 'Ten Categories' came into my hands. Whenever my teacher at Carthage and others who were reputed to be scholars mentioned this book, their cheeks would swell with self-importance, so that the title alone was enough to make me stand agape, as though I were poised over some wonderful divine mystery. I managed to read it and understand it without help, though I now ask myself what advantage I gained from doing so. Other people told me that they had understood it only with difficulty, after the most learned masters had not only explained it to them but also illustrated it with a wealth of diagrams. But when I discussed it with them, I found that they could tell me no more about it than I had already discovered by reading it on my own.

[. . .]

I read and understood by myself all the books that I could find on the so-called liberal arts, for in those days I was a good-for-nothing and a slave to sordid ambitions. But what advantage did I gain from them? I read them with pleasure, but I did not know the real source of such true and certain facts as they contained. I had my back to the light and my face was turned towards the things which it illumined, so that my eyes, by which I saw the things which stood in the light, were themselves in darkness. Without great difficulty and without need of a teacher I understood all that I read on the arts of rhetoric and logic, on geometry, music, and mathematics. You know this, O Lord my God, because if a man is quick to understand and his perception is keen, he has these gifts from you. But since I made no offering of them to you, it did me more harm than good to struggle to keep in my own power so large a part of what you had given to me and, instead of preserving my strength for you, to leave you and *go to a far country* to squander your gifts on loves that sold themselves for money. For what good to me was my ability, if I did not use it well? And ability I had, for until I tried to instruct others I did not realize that these subjects are very difficult to master, even for pupils who are studious and intelligent, and a student who could follow my instruction without faltering was reckoned a very fine scholar.

But what value did I gain from my reading as long as I thought that you, Lord God who are the Truth, were a bright, unbounded body and I a small piece broken from it? What utter distortion of the truth! Yet this was my belief; and I do not now blush to acknowledge, my God, the mercies you have shown to me, nor to call you to my aid, just as in those days I did not blush to declare my blasphemies aloud and snarl at you like a dog. What, then, was the value to me of my intelligence, which could take these subjects in its stride, and all those books, with their tangled problems, which I unravelled without the help of any human tutor, when in the doctrine of your love I was lost in the most hideous error and the vilest sacrilege? And was it so great a drawback to your faithful children that they were slower than I to understand such things? For they did not forsake you, but grew like fledglings in the safe nest of your Church, nourishing the wings of charity on the food of the faith that would save them.

O Lord our God, let *the shelter of your wings* give us hope. Protect us and uphold us. You will be the Support that upholds us from childhood till the hair on our heads is grey. When you are our strength we are strong, but when our strength is our own we are weak. In you our good abides for ever, and when we turn away from it we turn to evil. Let us come home at last to you, O Lord, for fear that we be lost. For in you our good abides and it has no blemish, since it is yourself. Nor do we fear that there is no home to which we can return. We fell from it; but our home is your eternity and it does not fall because we are away.

Book V

Accept my confessions, O Lord. They are a sacrifice offered by my tongue, for yours was the hand that fashioned it and yours the spirit that moved it to acknowledge you. Heal all my bones and let them say *Lord, there is none like you.*

If a man confesses to you, he does not reveal his inmost thoughts to you as though you did not know them. For the heart may shut itself away, but it cannot hide from your sight. Man's heart may be hard, but it cannot resist the touch of your hand. Whenever you will, your mercy or your punishment can make it relent, and just as none can hide away from the sun, *none can escape your burning heat.*

Let my soul praise you, so that it may show its love; and let it make avowal of your mercies, so that for these it may praise you. No part of your creation ever ceases to resound in praise of you. Man turns his lips to you in prayer and his spirit praises you. Animals too and lifeless things as well praise you through the lips of all who give them thought. For our souls lean for support upon the things which you have created, so that we may be lifted up to you from our weakness and use them to help us on our way to you who made them all so wonderfully. And in you we are remade and find true strength.

3

In the sight of my God I will describe the twenty-ninth year of my age.

A Manichean bishop named Faustus had recently arrived at Carthage. He was a great decoy of the devil and many people were trapped by his charming manner of speech. This I certainly admired, but I was beginning to distinguish between mere eloquence and the real truth, which I was so eager to learn. The Manichees talked so much about this man Faustus that I wanted to see what scholarly fare he would lay before me, and I did not care what words he used to garnish the dish. I had already heard that he was very well versed in all the higher forms of learning and particularly in the liberal sciences.

I had read a great many scientific books which were still alive in my memory. When I compared them with the tedious tales of the Manichees, it seemed to me that, of the two, the theories of the scientists were the more likely to be true. For *their thoughts could reach far enough to form a judgement about the world around them, though they found no trace of him who is Master of it. You, Lord, who are so high above us, yet look with favour on the humble, look on the proud too, but from far off.* You come close only to men who are humble at heart. The proud cannot find you, even though by dint of study they have skill to number stars and grains of sand, to measure the tracts of constellations and trace the paths of planets.

[. . .]

6

For almost the whole of those nine years during which my mind was unsettled and I was an aspirant of the Manichees, I awaited the coming of this man Faustus with the keenest expectation. Other members of the sect whom I happened to meet were unable to answer the questions I raised upon these subjects, but they assured me that once Faustus had arrived I had only to discuss them with him and he would have no difficulty in giving me a clear explanation of my queries and any other more difficult problems which I might put forward.

[. . .]

My long and eager expectation of Faustus's arrival was amply rewarded by the way in which he set about the task of disputation and the goodwill that he showed. The ease with which he found the right words to clothe his thoughts delighted me, and I was not the only one to applaud it, though perhaps I did so more than most. But I found it tiresome, when so many people assembled to hear him, not to be allowed to approach him with my difficulties and lay them before him in the friendly give-

and-take of conversation. As soon as the opportunity arose I and some of my friends claimed his attention at a time when a private discussion would not be inappropriate. I mentioned some of my doubts, but soon discovered that except for a rudimentary knowledge of literature he had no claims to scholarship. He had read some of Cicero's speeches, one or two books of Seneca, some poetry, and such books as had been written in good Latin by members of his sect. Besides his daily practice as a speaker, this reading was the basis of his eloquence, which derived extra charm and plausibility from his attractive personality and his ability to make good use of his mental powers.

[...]

7

As soon as it became clear to me that Faustus was quite uninformed about the subjects in which I had expected him to be an expert, I began to lose hope that he could lift the veil and resolve the problems which perplexed me. Of course, despite his ignorance of these matters he might still have been a truly pious man, provided he were not a Manichee. The Manichean books are full of the most tedious fictions about the sky and the stars, the sun and the moon. I badly wanted Faustus to compare these with the mathematical calculations which I had studied in other books, so that I might judge whether the Manichean theories were more likely to be true or, at least, equally probable, but I now began to realize that he could not give me a detailed explanation. When I suggested that we should consider these problems and discuss them together, he was certainly modest enough not to undertake the task. He knew that he did not know the answers to my questions and was not ashamed to admit it, for unlike many other talkative people whom I have had to endure, he would not try to teach me a lesson when he had nothing to say. He had a heart, and though his approach to you was mistaken, he was not without discretion. He was not entirely unaware of his limitations and did not want to enter rashly into an argument which might force him into a position which he could not possibly maintain and from which he could not easily withdraw. I liked him all the better for this, because modesty and candour are finer equipment for the mind than scientific knowledge of the kind that I wished to possess. I found that his attitude towards all the more difficult and abstruse questions was the same.

[. . .]

So it was that, unwittingly and without intent, Faustus who had been a deadly snare to many now began to release me from the trap in which I had been caught. For in the mystery of your providence, my God, your guiding hand did not desert me. Night and day my mother poured out her tears to you and offered her heart-blood in sacrifice for me, and in the most wonderful way you guided me. It was you who guided me, my God, for *man's feet stand firm, if the Lord is with him to prosper his journey*. What else can save us but your hand, remaking what you have made?

8

It was, then, by your guidance that I was persuaded to go to Rome and teach there the subjects which I taught at Carthage.

[. . .]

9

At Rome I was at once struck down by illness, which all but carried me off to hell loaded with all the evil that I had committed against you, against myself, and against other men, a host of grave offences over and above the bond of original sin, by which we *all have died with Adam*. You had not yet forgiven me any of these sins in Christ nor, on his cross, had he dissolved the enmity which my sins had earned me in your sight. How could he dissolve it on the cross if he were a mere phantom, as I believed? In so far, then, as I thought the death of his body unreal, the death of my own soul was real; and the life of my soul, because it doubted his death, was as false as the death of his flesh was true.

[. . .]

If I had died in that state, my mother's heart would never have recovered from the blow. Words cannot describe how dearly she loved me or how much greater was the anxiety she suffered for my spiritual birth than the physical pain she had endured in bringing me into the world. I cannot see how she could ever have recovered if I had died in that condition, for my death would have pierced the very heart of her love. And what would have become of all the fervent prayers which she offered so often and without fail? They would have come to you, nowhere but to you. But would you, O God of mercy, have despised the contrite and humble heart of that chaste and gentle widow, so ready to give alms, so full of humble reverence for your saints, who never let a day go by unless she had brought an offering to your altar, and never failed to come to your church twice every day, each morning and night, not to listen to empty tales and old wives' gossip, but so that she might hear the preaching of your word and you might listen to her prayers? Could you deny your help to her, when it was by your grace that she was what she was, or despise her tears, when she asked not for gold or silver or any fleeting, short-lived favour, but that the soul of her son might be saved? Never would you have done this, O Lord. No, you were there to hear her prayer and do all, in due order, as you had determined it was to be done. It could not be that you would have deceived her in the visions you sent her and the answers you gave to her prayers, both those that I have recorded and the others which I have not set down. All these signs she cherished in her faithful heart, and in her ceaseless prayers she laid them before you as though they were pledges signed by your hand. For, since *your mercy endures for ever*, by your promises you deign to become a debtor to those whom you release from every debt.

10

So it was that you healed my sickness. To the son of your servant you restored the health of his body, so that he might live to receive from you another far better and more certain kind of health.

[. . .]

12

I began actively to set about the business of teaching literature and public speaking, which was the purpose for which I had come to Rome. At first I taught in my house, where I collected a number of pupils who had heard of me, and through them my reputation began to grow. But I now realized that there were difficulties in Rome with which I had not had to contend in Africa. True enough, I found that there was no rioting by young hooligans, but I was told that at any moment a number of students would plot together to avoid paying their master his fees and would transfer in a body to another. They were quite unscrupulous, and justice meant nothing to them compared with the love of money. There was hatred for them in my heart, and it was not unselfish hatred, for I suppose that I hated them more for what I should have to suffer from them than for the wrong they might do to any teacher . . . For their warped and crooked minds I still hate students like these, but I love them too, hoping to teach them to mend their ways, so that they may learn to love their studies more than money and love you, their God, still more, for you are the Truth, the Source of good that does not fail, and the Peace of purest innocence. But in those days I was readier to dislike them for fear of the harm they might cause me than to hope that they would become good for your sake.

13

So, when the Prefect of Rome received a request from Milan to find a teacher of literature and elocution for the city, with a promise that travelling expenses would be charged to public funds, I applied for the appointment, armed with recommendations from my friends who were so fuddled with the Manichean rigmarole. This journey was to mean the end of my association with them, though none of us knew it at the time. Eventually Symmachus, who was then Prefect, set me a test to satisfy himself of my abilities and sent me to Milan.

In Milan I found your devoted servant the bishop Ambrose, who was known throughout the world as a man whom there were few to equal in goodness. At that time his gifted tongue never tired of dispensing the richness of your corn, the joy of your oil, and the sober intoxication of your wine. Unknown to me, it was you who led me to him, so that I might knowingly be led by him to you. This man of God received me like a father and, as bishop, told me how glad he was that I had come. My heart warmed to him, not at first as a teacher of the truth, which I had quite despaired of finding in your Church, but simply as a man who showed me kindness. I listened attentively when he preached to the people, though not with the proper intention; for my purpose was to judge for myself whether the reports of his powers as a speaker were accurate, or whether eloquence flowed from him more, or less, readily than I had been told. So while I paid the closest attention to the words he used, I was quite uninterested in the subject-matter and was even contemptuous of it. I was delighted with his charming delivery, but although he was a more learned speaker than Faustus, he had not the same soothing and gratifying manner. I am speaking only of his style for, as to content, there could be no comparison between the two. Faustus had lost his way among the fallacies of Manicheism, while Ambrose most surely taught the doctrine of salvation. But *your mercy is unknown to sinners* such as I was then, though step by step, unwittingly, I was coming closer to it.

14

For although I did not trouble to take what Ambrose said to heart, but only to listen to the manner in which he said it – this being the only paltry interest that remained to me now that I had lost hope that man could find the path that led to you – nevertheless his meaning, which I tried to ignore, found its way into my mind together with his words, which I admired so much. I could not keep the two apart, and while I was all ears to seize upon his eloquence, I also began to sense the truth of what he said, though only gradually. First of all it struck me that it was, after all, possible to vindicate his arguments. I began to believe that the Catholic faith, which I had thought impossible to defend against the objections of the Manichees, might fairly be maintained, especially since I had heard one passage after another in the Old Testament figuratively explained. These passages had been death to me when I took them literally, but once I had heard them explained in their spiritual meaning I began to blame myself for my despair, at least in so far as it had led me to suppose that it was quite impossible to counter people who hated and derided the law and the prophets. But I did not feel that I ought to follow the Catholic path simply because it too had its learned men, ready to vouch for it and never at a loss for sound arguments in answer to objections. On the other hand I did not think that my own beliefs should be condemned simply because an equally good case could be made out for either side. For I thought the Catholic side unbeaten but still not victorious.

Next I tried my utmost to find some certain proof which would convict the Manichees of falsehood. If I had been able to conceive of a spiritual substance, all their inventions would at once have been disproved and rejected from my mind. But this I could not do. However, the more I thought about the material world and the whole of nature, as far as we can be aware of it through our bodily senses, and the more I took stock of the various theories, the more I began to think that the opinions of the majority of the philosophers were most likely to be true. So, treating everything as a matter of doubt, as the Academics are generally supposed to do, and hovering between one doctrine and another, I made up my mind at least to leave the Manichees, for while I was in this state of indecision I did not think it right to remain in the sect now that I found the theories of some of the philosophers preferable. Nevertheless I utterly refused to entrust the healing of the maladies of my soul to these philosophers, because they ignored the saving name of Christ. I therefore decided to remain a catechumen in the Catholic Church, which was what my parents wanted, at least until I could clearly see a light to guide my steps.

Book VI

1

O God, *Hope of my youth*, where were you all this time? Where were you hiding from me? Were you not my Creator and was it not you who made me different from the beasts that walk on the earth and wiser than the birds that fly in the air? Yet I was walking on a treacherous path, in darkness. I was looking for you outside myself and I did not find the God of my own heart. I had reached the depths of the ocean. I had lost all faith and was in despair of finding the truth.

By now my mother had come to me, for her piety had given her strength to follow me over land and sea, facing all perils in the sure faith she had in you. When the ship was in danger, it was she who put heart into the crew, the very men to whom passengers unused to the sea turn for reassurance when they are alarmed. She promised them that they would make the land in safety, because you had given her this promise in a vision. And she found that I too was in grave danger because of my despair of discovering the truth. I told her that I was not a Catholic Christian, but at least I was no longer a Manichee. Yet she did not leap for joy as though this news were unexpected. In fact, to this extent, her anxiety for me had already been allayed. For in her prayers to you she wept for me as though I were dead, but she also knew that you would recall me to life. In her heart she offered me to you as though I were laid out on a bier, waiting for you to say to the widow's son, 'Young man, I say to you, stand up.' And he would get up and begin to speak, and you would give him back to his mother. So she felt no great surge of joy and her heart beat none the faster when she heard that the tears and the prayers which she had offered you day after day had at last, in great part, been rewarded. For I had been rescued from falsehood, even if I had not yet grasped the truth. Instead, because she was sure that if you had promised her all, you would also give her what remained to be given, she told me quite serenely, with her heart full of faith, that in Christ she believed that before she left this life she would see me a faithful Catholic. This was what she said to me. But to you, from whom all mercies spring, she poured out her tears and her prayers all the more fervently, begging you to speed your help and give me light in my darkness. She hurried all the more eagerly to church, where she listened with rapt attention to all that Ambrose said. For her his words were like *a spring of water within her, that flows continually to bring her everlasting life.* She loved him *as God's angel,* because she had learnt that it was through him that I had been led, for the time being, into a state of wavering uncertainty. She had no doubt that I must pass through this condition, which would lead me from sickness to health, but not before I had surmounted a still graver danger, much like that which doctors call the crisis.

5

From now on I began to prefer the Catholic teaching. The Church demanded that certain things should be believed even though they could not be proved, for if they could be proved, not all men could understand the proof, and some could not be proved at all. I thought that the Church was entirely honest in this and far less pretentious than the Manichees, who laughed at people who took things on faith, made rash promises of scientific knowledge, and then put forward a whole system of preposterous inventions which they expected their followers to believe on trust because they could not be proved. Then, O Lord, you laid your most gentle, most merciful finger on my heart and set my thoughts in order, for I began to realize that I believed countless things which I had never seen or which had taken place when I was not there to see – so many events in the history of the world, so many facts about places and towns which I had never seen, and so much that I believed on the word of friends or doctors or various other people. Unless we took these things on trust, we should accomplish absolutely nothing in this life. Most of all it came home to me how firm and unshakeable was the faith which told me who my parents were, because I could never have known this unless I believed what I was told. In this way you made me understand that I ought not to find fault with those who believed your Bible, which you have established with such great authority amongst almost all the nations of the earth, but with those who did not believe it; and that I ought to pay no attention to people who asked me how I could be sure that the Scriptures were delivered to mankind by the Spirit of the one true God who can tell no lie. It was precisely this that I most needed to believe, because in all the conflicting books of philosophy which I had read no misleading proposition, however contentious, had been able, even for one moment, to wrest from me my belief in your existence and in your right to govern human affairs; and this despite the fact that I had no knowledge of what you are.

My belief that you existed and that our well-being was in your hands was sometimes strong, sometimes weak, but I always held to it even though I knew neither what I ought to think about your substance nor which way would lead me to you or lead me back to you. And so, since we are too weak to discover the truth by reason alone and for this reason need the authority of sacred books, I began to believe that you would never have invested the Bible with such conspicuous authority in every land unless you had intended it to be the means by which we should look for you and believe in you. As for the passages which had previously struck me as absurd, now that I had heard reasonable explanations of many of them I regarded them as of the nature of profound mysteries; and it seemed to me all the more right that the authority of Scripture should be respected and accepted with the purest faith, because while all can read it with ease, it also has a deeper meaning in which its great secrets are locked away. Its plain language and simple style make it accessible to everyone, and yet it absorbs the attention of the learned. By this means it gathers all men in the wide sweep of its net, and some pass safely through the narrow mesh and come to you. They are not many, but they would be fewer still if it were not that this book stands out alone on so high a peak of authority and yet draws so great a throng in the embrace of its holy humility.

[. . .]

13

I was being urged incessantly to marry, and had already made my proposal and been accepted. My mother had done all she could to help, for it was her hope that, once I was married, I should be washed clean of my sins by the saving waters of baptism. She was delighted that, day by day, I was becoming more fitted for baptism, and in my acceptance of the faith she saw the answer to her prayers and the fulfilment of your promises. At my request and by her own desire she daily beseeched you with heartfelt prayers to send her some revelation in a vision about my future marriage, but this you would not do. She had some vague and fanciful dreams, which were the result of her preoccupation with these thoughts, and when she told me about them, she treated them as of no importance and did not speak with the assurance that she always had when you sent her visions. She always said that by some sense, which she could not describe in words, she was able to distinguish between your revelations and her own natural dreams. All the same, the plans for my marriage were pushed ahead and the girl's parents were asked for their consent. She was nearly two years too young for marriage, but I liked her well enough and was content to wait.

15

Meanwhile I was sinning more and more. The woman with whom I had been living was torn from my side as an obstacle to my marriage and this was a blow which crushed my heart to bleeding, because I loved her dearly. She went back to Africa, vowing never to give herself to any other man, and left with me the son whom she had borne me. But I was too unhappy and too weak to imitate this example set me by a woman. I was impatient at the delay of two years which had to pass before the girl whom I had asked to marry became my wife, and because I was more a slave of lust than a true lover of marriage, I took another mistress, without the sanction of wedlock. This meant that the disease of my soul would continue unabated, in fact it would be aggravated, and under the watch and ward of uninterrupted habit it would persist into the state of marriage. Furthermore the wound that I had received when my first mistress was wrenched away showed no signs of healing. At first the pain was sharp and searing, but then the wound began to fester, and though the pain was duller there was all the less hope of a cure.

16

Praise and honour be yours, O Fountain of mercy! As my misery grew worse and worse, you came the closer to me. Though I did not know it, your hand was poised ready to lift me from the mire and wash me clean. Nothing prevented me from plunging still deeper into the gulf of carnal pleasure except the fear of death and your judgement to come. Through all my changing opinions this fear never left my heart.

[. . .]

What crooked paths I trod! What dangers threatened my soul when it rashly hoped that by abandoning you it would find something better! Whichever way it turned, on front or back or sides, it lay on a bed that was hard, for in you alone the soul can rest. You are there to free us from the misery of error which leads us astray, to set us on your own path and to comfort us by saying, 'Run on, for I shall hold you up. I shall lead you and carry you on to the end.'

Book VII

1

By now my adolescence, with all its shameful sins, was dead. I was approaching mature manhood, but the older I grew, the more disgraceful was my self-delusion. I could imagine no kind of substance except such as is normally seen by the eye. But I did not think of you, my God, in the shape of a human body, for I had rejected this idea ever since I had first begun to study philosophy, and I was glad to find that our spiritual mother, your Catholic Church, also rejected such beliefs. But I did not know how else to think of you.

I was only a man, and a weak man at that, but I tried to think of you as the supreme God, the only God, the true God. With all my heart I believed that you could never suffer decay or hurt or change, for although I did not know how or why this should be, I understood with complete certainty that what is subject to decay is inferior to that which is not, and without hesitation I placed that which cannot be harmed above that which can, and I saw that what remains constant is better than that which is changeable. My heart was full of bitter protests against the creations of my imagination, and this single truth was the only weapon with which I could try to drive from my mind's eye all the unclean images which swarmed before it. But hardly had I brushed them aside than, in the flicker of an eyelid, they crowded upon me again, forcing themselves upon my sight and clouding my vision, so that although I did not imagine you in the shape of a human body, I could not free myself from the thought that you were some kind of bodily substance extended in space, either permeating the world or diffused in infinity beyond it. This substance I thought of as something not subject to decay or harm or variation and therefore better than any that might suffer corruption or damage or change. I reasoned in this way because, if I tried to imagine something without dimensions of space, it seemed to me that nothing, absolutely nothing, remained, not even a void. For if a body were removed from the space which it occupied, and that space remained empty of any body whatsoever, whether of earth, water, air, or sky, there would still remain an empty space. Nothing would be there, but it would still be a space.

[. . .]

So I thought of you too, O Life of my life, as a great being with dimensions extending everywhere, throughout infinite space, permeating the whole mass of the world and reaching in all directions beyond it without limit, so that the earth and the sky and all creation were full of you and their limits were within you, while you had no limits at all. For the air, that is, the atmosphere which covers the earth, is a material body, but it does not block out the light of the sun. The light passes through it and penetrates it, not by breaking it or splitting it, but by filling it completely. In the same way I imagined that you were able to pass through material bodies, not only the air and the sky and the sea, but also the earth, and that you could penetrate to all their parts, the greatest and the smallest alike, so that they were filled with your presence, and by this unseen force you ruled over all that you had created, from within and from without.

This was the theory to which I held, because I could imagine you in no other way. But it was a false theory. For if it were true, it would mean that a greater part of the earth would contain a greater part of you, and a smaller part less in proportion. Everything would be filled with your presence, but in such a way that the body of an elephant would contain more of you than the body of a sparrow, because the one is larger than the other and occupies more space. So you would distribute your parts piecemeal among the parts of the world, to each more or less according to its size. This, of course, is quite untrue. But at that time you had not yet given me light in my darkness.

3

But although I declared and firmly believed that you, our Lord God, the true God who made not only our souls but also our bodies and not only our souls and bodies but all things, living and inanimate, as well, although I believed that you were free from corruption or mutation or any degree of change, I still could not find a clear explanation, without complications, of the cause of evil. Whatever the cause might be, I saw that it was not to be found in any theory that would oblige me to believe that the immutable God was mutable. If I believed this, I should myself become a cause of evil, the very thing which I was trying to discover. So I continued the search with some sense of relief, because I was quite sure that the theories of the Manichees were wrong. I repudiated these people with all my heart, because I could see that while they were inquiring into the origin of evil they were full of evil themselves, since they preferred to think that yours was a substance that could suffer evil rather than that theirs was capable of committing it.

I was told that we do evil because we choose to do so of our own free will, and suffer it because your justice rightly demands that we should. I did my best to understand this, but I could not see it clearly. I tried to raise my mental perceptions out of the abyss which engulfed them, but I sank back into it once more. Again and again I tried, but always I sank back. One thing lifted me up into the light of your day. It was that I knew that I had a will, as surely as I knew that there was life in me. When I chose to do something or not to do it, I was quite certain that it was my own self, and not some other person, who made this act of will, so that I was on the point of understanding that herein lay the cause of my sin. If I did anything against my will, it seemed to me to be something which happened to me rather than something which I did, and I looked upon it not as a fault, but as a punishment. And because I thought of you as a just God, I admitted at once that your punishments were not unjust.

But then I would ask myself once more: 'Who made me? Surely it was my God, who is not only good but Goodness itself. How, then, do I come to possess a will that can choose to do wrong and refuse to do good, thereby providing a just reason why I should be punished? Who put this will into me? Who sowed this seed of bitterness in me, when all that I am was made by my God, who is Sweetness itself? If it was the devil who put it there, who made the devil? If he was a good angel who became a devil because of his own wicked will, how did he come to possess the wicked will which made him a devil, when the Creator, who is entirely good, made him a good angel and nothing else?'

[. . .]

12

It was made clear to me also that even those things which are subject to decay are good. If they were of the supreme order of goodness, they could not become corrupt; but neither could they become corrupt unless they were in some way good. For if they were supremely good, it would not be possible for them to be corrupted. On the other hand, if they were entirely without good, there would be nothing in them that could become corrupt. For corruption is harmful, but unless it diminished what is good, it could do no harm. The conclusion then must be either that corruption does no harm – which is not possible; or that everything which is corrupted is deprived of good – which is beyond doubt. But if they are deprived of all good, they will not exist at all. For if they still exist but can no longer be corrupted, they will be better than they were before, because they now continue their existence in an incorruptible state. But could anything be more preposterous than to say that things are made better by being deprived of all good?

So we must conclude that if things are deprived of all good, they cease altogether to be; and this means that as long as they are, they are good. Therefore, whatever is, is good; and evil, the origin of which I was trying to find, is not a substance, because if it were a substance, it would be good. For either it would be an incorruptible substance of the supreme order of goodness, or it would be a corruptible substance which would not be corruptible unless it were good. So it became obvious to me that all that you have made is good, and that there are no substances whatsoever that were not made by you. And because you did not make them all equal, each single thing is good and collectively they are very good, for our God made his whole creation *very good*.

17

I was astonished that although I now loved you and not some phantom in your place, I did not persist in enjoyment of my God. Your beauty drew me to you, but soon I was dragged away from you by my own weight and in dismay I plunged again into the things of this world. The weight I carried was the habit of the flesh. But your memory remained with me and I had no doubt at all that you were the one to whom I should cling, only I was not yet able to cling to you. For *ever the soul is weighed down by a mortal body, earth-bound cell that clogs the manifold activity of its thought*. I was most certain, too, that *from the foundations of the world men have caught sight of your invisible nature, your eternal power, and your divineness, as they are known through your creatures*. For I wondered how it was that I could appreciate beauty in material things on earth or in the heavens, and what it was that enabled me to make correct decisions about things that are subject to change and to rule that one thing ought to be like this, another like that. I wondered how it was that I was able to judge them in this way, and I realized that above my own mind, which was liable to change, there was the never changing, true eternity of truth. So, step by step, my thoughts moved on from the consideration of material things to the soul, which perceives things through the senses of the body, and then to the soul's inner power, to which the bodily senses communicate external facts. Beyond this dumb animals cannot go. The next stage is the power of reason, to which the facts communicated by the bodily senses are submitted for judgement.

This power of reason, realizing that in me it too was liable to change, led me on to consider the source of its own understanding. It withdrew my thoughts from their normal course and drew back from the confusion of images which pressed upon it, so that it might discover what light it was that had been shed upon it when it proclaimed for certain that what was immutable was

better than that which was not, and how it had come to
know the immutable itself. For unless, by some means,
it had known the immutable, it could not possibly have
been certain that it was preferable to the mutable. And
so, in an instant of awe, my mind attained to the sight
of the God who IS. Then, at last, *I caught sight of your
invisible nature, as it is known through your creatures*. But
I had no strength to fix my gaze upon them. In my
weakness I recoiled and fell back into my old ways,
carrying with me nothing but the memory of something
that I loved and longed for, as though I had sensed the
fragrance of the fare but was not yet able to eat it.

18

I began to search for a means of gaining the strength I
needed to enjoy you, but I could not find this means
until I embraced the *mediator between God and men, Jesus
Christ, who is a man, like them*, and also *rules as God over
all things, blessed for ever*. He was calling to me and saying
I am the way; I am truth and life. He it was who united
with our flesh that food which I was too weak to take;
for *the Word was made flesh* so that your Wisdom, by
which you created all things, might be milk to suckle us
in infancy. For I was not humble enough to conceive of
the humble Jesus Christ as my God, nor had I learnt
what lesson his human weakness was meant to teach.
The lesson is that your Word, the eternal Truth, which
far surpasses even the higher parts of your creation,
raises up to himself all who subject themselves to him.

From the clay of which we are made he built for himself a lowly house in this world below, so that by this means he might cause those who were to be made subject to him to abandon themselves and come over to his side. He would cure them of the pride that swelled up in their hearts and would nurture love in its place, so that they should no longer stride ahead confident in themselves, but might realize their own weakness when at their feet they saw God himself, enfeebled by sharing this garment of our mortality. And at last, from weariness, they would cast themselves down upon his humanity, and when it rose they too would rise.

Book VIII

6

O Lord, my Helper and my Redeemer, I shall now tell and confess to the glory of your name how you released me from the fetters of lust which held me so tightly shackled and from my slavery to the things of this world [. . .]

One day when for some reason that I cannot recall Nebridius was not with us, Alypius and I were visited at our house by a fellow-countryman of ours from Africa, a man named Ponticianus, who held a high position in the Emperor's household. He had some request to make of us and we sat down to talk. He happened to notice a book lying on a table used for games, which was near where we were sitting. He picked it up and opened it and was greatly surprised to find that it contained Paul's epistles, for he had supposed that it was one of the books which used to tax all my strength as a teacher. Then he smiled and looked at me and said how glad he was, and how surprised, to find this book, and no others, there before my eyes. He of course was a Christian and a faithful servant to you, our God. Time and again he knelt before you in church repeating his prayers and lingering over them. When I told him that I studied Paul's writings with the greatest attention, he began to tell us the story of Antony, the Egyptian monk, whose name was held in high honour by your servants, although Alypius and I had never heard it until then. When Ponticianus realized this, he went into greater detail, wishing to instil some knowledge of this great man into our ignorant minds, for he was very surprised that we had not heard of him. For our part, we too were astonished to hear of the wonders you had worked so recently, almost in our own times, and witnessed by so many, in the true faith and in the Catholic Church. In fact all three of us were amazed, Alypius and I because the story we heard was so remarkable, and Ponticianus because we had not heard it before.

After this he went on to tell us of the groups of monks in the monasteries, of their way of life that savours of your sweetness, and of the fruitful wastes of the desert. All of this was new to us. There was a monastery at Milan also, outside the walls, full of good brethren under the care of Ambrose, but we knew nothing of this either. Ponticianus continued to talk and we listened in silence. Eventually he told us of the time when he and three of his companions were at Trêves. One afternoon, while the Emperor was watching the games in the circus, they went out to stroll in the gardens near the city walls. They became separated into two groups, Ponticianus and one of the others remaining together while the other two went off by themselves. As they wandered on, the second pair came to a house which was the home of some servants of yours, men poor in spirit, to whom the kingdom of heaven belongs. In the house they found a book containing the life of Antony. One of them began to read it and was so fascinated and thrilled by the story that even before he had finished reading he conceived the idea of taking upon himself the same kind of life and abandoning his career in the world – both he and his friend were officials in the service of the State – in order to become your servant. All at once he was filled with the love of holiness. Angry with himself and full of remorse, he looked at his friend and said, 'What do we hope to gain by all the efforts we make? What are we looking for? What is our purpose in serving the State? Can we hope for anything better at Court than to be the Emperor's friends? Even so, surely our position would be precarious and exposed to much danger? We shall meet it at every turn, only to reach another danger which is greater still. And how long is it to be before we reach it? But if I wish, I can become the friend of God at this very moment.'

After saying this he turned back to the book, labouring under the pain of the new life that was taking birth in him. He read on and in his heart, where you alone could see, a change was taking place. His mind was being divested of the world, as could presently be seen. For while he was reading, his heart leaping and turning in his breast, a cry broke from him as he saw the better course and determined to take it. Your servant now, he said to his friend, 'I have torn myself free from all our ambitions and have decided to serve God. From this very moment, here and now, I shall start to serve him. If you will not follow my lead, do not stand in my way.' The other answered that he would stand by his comrade, for such service was glorious and the reward was great.

So these two, now your servants, built their tower at the cost which had to be paid, that is, at the cost of giving up all they possessed and following you.

At this moment Ponticianus and the man who had been walking with him in another part of the garden arrived at the house, looking for their friends. Now that they had found them they said that it was time to go home, as the daylight was beginning to fade. But the other two told them of the decision they had made and what they proposed to do. They explained what had made them decide to take this course and how they had agreed upon it, and they asked their friends, if they would not join them, at least not to put obstacles in their way. Ponticianus said that he and the other man did not change their old ways, but they were moved to tears for their own state of life. In all reverence they congratulated the others and commended themselves to their prayers. Then they went back to the palace, burdened with hearts that were bound to this earth; but the others remained in the house and their hearts were fixed upon heaven. Both these men were under a promise of marriage, but once the two women heard what had happened, they too dedicated their virginity to you.

7

This was what Ponticianus told us. But while he was speaking, O Lord, you were turning me around to look at myself. For I had placed myself behind my own back, refusing to see myself. You were setting me before my own eyes so that I could see how sordid I was, how deformed and squalid, how tainted with ulcers and sores. I saw it all and stood aghast, but there was no place where I could escape from myself. If I tried to turn my eyes away they fell on Ponticianus, still telling his tale, and in this way you brought me face to face with myself once more, forcing me upon my own sight so that I should see my wickedness and loathe it. I had known it all along, but I had always pretended that it was something different. I had turned a blind eye and forgotten it.

But now, the more my heart warmed to those two men as I heard how they had made the choice that was to save them by giving themselves up entirely to your care, the more bitterly I hated myself in comparison with them. Many years of my life had passed – twelve, unless I am wrong – since I had read Cicero's *Hortensius* at the age of nineteen and it had inspired me to study philosophy. But I still postponed my renunciation of this world's joys, which would have left me free to look for that other happiness, the very search for which, let alone its discovery, I ought to have prized above the discovery of all human treasures and kingdoms or the ability to enjoy all the pleasures of the body at a mere nod of the head. As a youth I had been woefully at fault, particularly in early adolesence. I had prayed to you for chastity and said 'Give me chastity and continence, but not yet.' For I was afraid that you would answer my prayer at once and cure me too soon of the disease of lust, which I wanted satisfied, not quelled. I had wandered on along the road of vice in the sacrilegious superstition of the Manichees, not because I thought that it was right, but because I preferred it to the Christian belief, which I did not explore as I ought but opposed out of malice.

[. . .]

All the time that Ponticianus was speaking my conscience gnawed away at me like this. I was overcome by burning shame, and when he had finished his tale and completed the business for which he had come, he went away and I was left to my own thoughts. I made all sorts of accusations against myself. I cudgelled my soul and belaboured it with reasons why it should follow me now that I was trying so hard to follow you. But it fought back. It would not obey and yet could offer no excuse. All its old arguments were exhausted and had been shown to be false. It remained silent and afraid, for as much as the loss of life itself it feared the stanching of the flow of habit, by which it was wasting away to death.

8

My inner self was a house divided against itself. In the heat of the fierce conflict which I had stirred up against my soul in our common abode, my heart, I turned upon Alypius. My looks betrayed the commotion in my mind as I exclaimed, 'What is the matter with us? What is the meaning of this story? These men have not had our schooling, yet they stand up and storm the gates of heaven while we, for all our learning, lie here grovelling in this world of flesh and blood! Is it because they have led the way that we are ashamed to follow? Is it not worse to hold back?'

[. . .]

There was a small garden attached to the house where we lodged. We were free to make use of it as well as the rest of the house because our host, the owner of the house, did not live there. I now found myself driven by the tumult in my breast to take refuge in this garden, where no one could interrupt that fierce struggle, in which I was my own contestant, until it came to its conclusion. What the conclusion was to be you knew, O Lord, but I did not. Meanwhile I was beside myself with madness that would bring me sanity. I was dying a death that would bring me life. I knew the evil that was in me, but the good that was soon to be born in me I did not know. So I went out into the garden and Alypius followed at my heels. His presence was no intrusion on my solitude, and how could he leave me in that state? We sat down as far as possible from the house. I was frantic, overcome by violent anger with myself for not accepting your will and entering into your covenant. Yet in my bones I knew that this was what I ought to do. In my heart of hearts I praised it to the skies. And to reach this goal I needed no chariot or ship. I need not even walk as far as I had come from the house to the place where we sat, for to make the journey, and to arrive safely, no more was required than an act of will. But it must be a resolute and whole-hearted act of the will, not some lame wish which I kept turning over and over in my mind, so that it had to wrestle with itself, part of it trying to rise, part falling to the ground.

[. . .]

11

This was the nature of my sickness. I was in torment, reproaching myself more bitterly than ever as I twisted and turned in my chain. I hoped that my chain might be broken once and for all, because it was only a small thing that held me now. All the same it held me. And you, O Lord, never ceased to watch over my secret heart. In your stern mercy you lashed me with the twin scourge of fear and shame in case I should give way once more and the worn and slender remnant of my chain should not be broken but gain new strength and bind me all the faster. In my heart I kept saying 'Let it be now, let it be now!', and merely by saying this I was on the point of making the resolution. I was on the point of making it, but I did not succeed. Yet I did not fall back into my old state. I stood on the brink of resolution, waiting to take fresh breath. I tried again and came a little nearer to my goal, and then a little nearer still, so that I could almost reach out and grasp it. But I did not reach it. I could not reach out to it or grasp it, because I held back from the step by which I should die to death and become alive to life. My lower instincts, which had taken firm hold of me, were stronger than the higher, which were untried.

And the closer I came to the moment which was to mark the great change in me, the more I shrank from it in horror. But it did not drive me back or turn me from my purpose: it merely left me hanging in suspense.

[. . .]

12

I probed the hidden depths of my soul and wrung its pitiful secrets from it, and when I mustered them all before the eyes of my heart, a great storm broke within me, bringing with it a great deluge of tears. I stood up and left Alypius so that I might weep and cry to my heart's content, for it occurred to me that tears were best shed in solitude. I moved away far enough to avoid being embarrassed even by his presence. He must have realized what my feelings were, for I suppose I had said something and he had known from the sound of my voice that I was ready to burst into tears. So I stood up and left him where we had been sitting, utterly bewildered. Somehow I flung myself down beneath a fig tree and gave way to the tears which now streamed from my eyes, the sacrifice that is acceptable to you. I had much to say to you, my God, not in these very words but in this strain: *Lord, will you never be content? Must we always taste your vengeance? Forget the long record of our sins.* For I felt that I was still the captive of my sins, and in my misery I kept crying 'How long shall I go on saying "tomorrow, tomorrow"? Why not now? Why not make an end of my ugly sins at this moment?'

I was asking myself these questions, weeping all the while with the most bitter sorrow in my heart, when all at once I heard the sing-song voice of a child in a nearby house. Whether it was the voice of a boy or a girl I cannot say, but again and again it repeated the refrain 'Take it and read, take it and read'. At this I looked up, thinking hard whether there was any kind of game in which children used to chant words like these, but I could not remember ever hearing them before. I stemmed my flood of tears and stood up, telling myself that this could only be a divine command to open my book of Scripture and read the first passage on which my eyes should fall. For I had heard the story of Antony, and I remembered how he had happened to go into a church while the Gospel was being read and had taken it as a counsel addressed to himself when he heard the words *Go home and sell all that belongs to you. Give it to the poor, and so the treasure you have shall be in heaven; then come back and follow me.* By this divine pronouncement he had at once been converted to you.

So I hurried back to the place where Alypius was sitting, for when I stood up to move away I had put down the book containing Paul's Epistles. I seized it and opened it, and in silence I read the first passage on which my eyes fell: *Not in revelling and drunkenness, not in lust and wantonness, not in quarrels and rivalries. Rather, arm yourselves with the Lord Jesus Christ; spend no more thought on nature and nature's appetites.* I had no wish to read more and no need to do so. For in an instant, as I came to the end of the sentence, it was as though the light of confidence flooded into my heart and all the darkness of doubt was dispelled.

I marked the place with my finger or by some other sign and closed the book. My looks now were quite calm as I told Alypius what had happened to me. He too told me what he had been feeling, which of course I did not know. He asked to see what I had read. I showed it to him and he read on beyond the text which I had read. I did not know what followed, but it was this: *Find room among you for a man of over-delicate conscience*. Alypius applied this to himself and told me so. This admonition was enough to give him strength, and without suffering the distress of hesitation he made his resolution and took this good purpose to himself. And it very well suited his moral character, which had long been far, far better than my own.

Then we went in and told my mother, who was overjoyed. And when we went on to describe how it had all happened, she was jubilant with triumph and glorified you, *who are powerful enough, and more than powerful enough, to carry out your purpose beyond all our hopes and dreams*. For she saw that you had granted her far more than she used to ask in her tearful prayers and plaintive lamentations. You converted me to yourself, so that I no longer desired a wife or placed any hope in this world but stood firmly upon the rule of faith, where you had shown me to her in a dream so many years before. And you *turned her sadness into rejoicing*, into joy far fuller than her dearest wish, far sweeter and more chaste than any she had hoped to find in children begotten of my flesh.

Book IX

Knowing that you were watching me I thought it best to retire quietly from the market where I sold the services of my tongue rather than make an abrupt and sensational departure. I intended that young pupils who gave no thought to your law or your peace, but only to lies and the insane warfare of the courts, should no longer buy from my lips any weapon to arm their madness. Luckily there were now only a few days left before the autumn holidays, and I decided to bear with this delay and withdraw at the proper time. Now that I had been redeemed by you I had no intention of offering myself for sale again. This plan was known to you, but no man knew of it except our closest friends. We had agreed that it should not be made generally known, although, as we climbed up from the valley of tears, singing the song of ascent, you had given us sharp arrows and burning coals to use against any cunning tongues that might speak against us under the pretence of giving good advice and devour us with their love, just as men devour food for which they have a liking.

[. . .]

6

When the time came for me to hand in my name for baptism, we left the country and went back to Milan. It was Alypius's wish to be reborn in you at the same time. He was already endued with the humility which fits a man for your sacraments, and he had subjected his body to such stern discipline that he would even walk barefoot on the icy soil of Italy, a thing which few would venture to do. With us we took the boy Adeodatus, my natural son born of my sin. You had given him every gift. Although he was barely fifteen, there were many learned and respected men who were not his equals in intelligence. I acknowledge that he had his gifts from you, O Lord my God, who are the Creator of all and have great power to reshape our deformities, for there was nothing of mine in that boy except my sin. It was you too, and none other, who had inspired us to bring him up as you would have him. These were your gifts and I acknowledge them.

[. . .]

We made him our companion, in your grace no younger than ourselves. Together we were ready to begin our schooling in your ways. We were baptized, and all anxiety over the past melted away from us. The days were all too short, for I was lost in wonder and joy, meditating upon your far-reaching providence for the salvation of the human race. The tears flowed from me when I heard your hymns and canticles, for the sweet singing of your Church moved me deeply. The music surged in my ears, truth seeped into my heart, and my feelings of devotion overflowed, so that the tears streamed down. But they were tears of gladness.

8

You, O God, who bring men of one mind to live together, brought a young man from our own town, named Evodius, to join our company. He had been converted and baptized before us, while he was employed as a government officer, but he had given up the service of the State and entered upon yours. He remained with us and we intended to live together in the devout life which we proposed to lead. We discussed where we could most usefully serve you and together we set out to return to Africa. While we were at Ostia, at the mouth of the Tiber, my mother died.

There are many things which I do not set down in this book, since I am pressed for time. My God, I pray you to accept my confessions and also the gratitude I bear you for all the many things which I pass over in silence. But I will omit not a word that my mind can bring to birth concerning your servant, my mother. In the flesh she brought me to birth in this world: in her heart she brought me to birth in your eternal light. It is not of her gifts that I shall speak, but of the gifts you gave to her. For she was neither her own maker nor her own teacher. It was you who made her, and neither her father nor her mother knew what kind of woman their daughter would grow up to be. It was by Christ's teaching, by the guidance of your only Son, that she was brought up to honour and obey you in one of those good Christian families which form the body of your Church [. . .]

10

Not long before the day on which she was to leave this life – you knew which day it was to be, O Lord, though we did not – my mother and I were alone, leaning from a window which overlooked the garden in the courtyard of the house where we were staying at Ostia. We were waiting there after our long and tiring journey, away from the crowd, to refresh ourselves before our sea-voyage. I believe that what I am going to tell happened through the secret working of your providence. For we were talking alone together and our conversation was serene and joyful. *We had forgotten what we had left behind and were intent on what lay before us.* In the presence of Truth, which is yourself, we were wondering what the eternal life of the saints would be like, that life which *no eye has seen, no ear has heard, no human heart conceived.* But we laid the lips of our hearts to the heavenly stream that flows from your fountain, *the source of all life* which is *in you,* so that as far as it was in our power to do so we might be sprinkled with its waters and in some sense reach an understanding of this great mystery.

Our conversation led us to the conclusion that no

bodily pleasure, however great it might be and whatever earthly light might shed lustre upon it, was worthy of comparison, or even of mention, beside the happiness of the life of the saints. As the flame of love burned stronger in us and raised us higher towards the eternal God, our thoughts ranged over the whole compass of material things in their various degrees, up to the heavens themselves, from which the sun and the moon and the stars shine down upon the earth. Higher still we climbed, thinking and speaking all the while in wonder at all that you have made. At length we came to our own souls and passed beyond them to that place of everlasting plenty, where you feed Israel for ever with the food of truth. There life is that Wisdom by which all these things that we know are made, all things that ever have been and all that are yet to be. But that Wisdom is not made: it is as it has always been and as it will be for ever – or, rather, I should not say that it *has been* or *will be*, for it simply *is*, because eternity is not in the past or in the future. And while we spoke of the eternal Wisdom, longing for it and straining for it with all the strength of our hearts, for one fleeting instant we reached out and touched it. Then with a sigh, leaving *our spiritual harvest* bound to it, we returned to the sound of our own speech, in which each word has a beginning and an ending – far, far different from your Word, our Lord, who abides in himself for ever, yet never grows old and gives new life to all things.

[. . .]

This was the purport of our talk, though we did not speak in these precise words or exactly as I have reported them. Yet you know, O Lord, that as we talked that day, the world, for all its pleasures, seemed a paltry place compared with the life that we spoke of. And then my mother said, 'My son, for my part I find no further pleasure in this life. What I am still to do or why I am here in the world, I do not know, for I have no more to hope for on this earth. There was one reason, and one alone, why I wished to remain a little longer in this life, and that was to see you a Catholic Christian before I died. God has granted my wish and more besides, for I now see you as his servant, spurning such happiness as the world can give. What is left for me to do in this world?'

11

I scarcely remember what answer I gave her. It was about five days after this, or not much more, that she took to her bed with a fever. One day during her illness she had a fainting fit and lost consciousness for a short time. We hurried to her bedside, but she soon regained consciousness and looked up at my brother and me as we stood beside her. With a puzzled look she asked 'Where was I?' Then watching us closely as we stood there speechless with grief, she said 'You will bury your mother here.' I said nothing, trying hard to hold back my tears, but my brother said something to the effect that he wished for her sake that she would die in her own country, not abroad. When she heard this, she looked at him anxiously and her eyes reproached him for his worldly thoughts. She turned to me and said, 'See how he talks!' and then, speaking to both of us, she went on, 'It does not matter where you bury my body. Do not let that worry you! All I ask of you is that, wherever you may be, you should remember me at the altar of the Lord.'

[. . .]

And so on the ninth day of her illness, when she was fifty-six and I was thirty-three, her pious and devoted soul was set free from the body.

13

Now that my soul has recovered from that wound, in which perhaps I was guilty of too much worldly affection, tears of another sort stream from my eyes. They are tears which I offer to you, my God, for your handmaid. They flow from a spirit which trembles at the thought of the dangers which await every soul that *has died with Adam*. For although she was alive in Christ even before her soul was parted from the body, and her faith and the good life she led resounded to the glory of your name, yet I cannot presume to say that from the time when she was reborn in baptism no word contrary to your commandments ever fell from her lips. Your Son, the Truth, has said: *Any man who says to his brother, You fool, must answer for it in hell fire*, and however praiseworthy a man's life may be, it will go hard with him if you lay aside your mercy when you come to examine it. But you do not search out our faults ruthlessly, and because of this we hope and believe that one day we shall find a place with you. Yet if any man makes a list of his deserts, what would it be but a list of your gifts? If only men would know themselves for what they are! If only *they who boast would make their boast in the Lord!*

And so, my Glory and my Life, God of my heart, I will lay aside for a while all the good deeds which my mother did. For them I thank you, but now I pray to you for her sins. Hear me through your Son, who hung on the cross and now *sits at your right hand and pleads for us*, for he is the true medicine of our wounds. I know that my mother always acted with mercy and that she forgave others with all her heart when they trespassed against her. Forgive her too, O Lord, if ever she trespassed against you in all the long years of her life after baptism. Forgive her, I beseech you; *do not call her to account. Let your mercy give your judgement an honourable welcome*, for your words are true and you have promised mercy to the merciful. If they are merciful, it is by your gift; and *you will show pity on those whom you pity; you will show mercy where you are merciful.*

[. . .]

Let her rest in peace with her husband. He was her first husband and she married no other after him. She served him, *yielding you a harvest*, so that in the end she also won him for you. O my Lord, my God, inspire your servants my brothers – they are your sons and my masters, whom I serve with heart and voice and pen – inspire those of them who read this book to remember Monica, your servant, at your altar and with her Patricius, her husband, who died before her, by whose bodies you brought me into this life, though how it was I do not know. With pious hearts let them remember those who were not only my parents in this light that fails, but were also my brother and sister, subject to you, our Father, in our Catholic mother the Church, and will be my fellow citizens in the eternal Jerusalem for which your people sigh throughout their pilgrimage, from the time when they set out until the time when they return to you. So it shall be that the last request that my mother made to me shall be granted in the prayers of the many who read my confessions more fully than in mine alone.

Book X

2

O Lord, the depths of man's conscience lie bare before your eyes. Could anything of mine remain hidden from you, even if I refused to confess it? I should only be shielding my eyes from seeing you, not hiding myself from you. But now that I have the evidence of my own misery to prove to me how displeasing I am to myself, you are my light and my joy. It is you whom I love and desire, so that I am ashamed of myself and cast myself aside and choose you instead, and I please neither you nor myself except in you.

So, O Lord, all that I am is laid bare before you. I have declared how it profits me to confess to you. And I make my confession, not in words and sounds made by the tongue alone, but with the voice of my soul and in my thoughts which cry aloud to you. Your ear can hear them. For when I am sinful, if I am displeased with myself, this is a confession that I make to you; and when I am good, if I do not claim the merit for myself, this too is confession. For you, O Lord, *give your benediction to the just*, but first *you make a just man of the sinner*. And so my confession is made both silently in your sight, my God, and aloud as well, because even though my tongue utters no sound, my heart cries to you. For whatever good I

may speak to men you have heard it before in my heart,
and whatever good you hear in my heart, you have first
spoken to me yourself.

4

But what good do they hope will be done if they listen
to what I say? Is it that they wish to join with me in
thanking you, when they hear how close I have come to
you by your grace, and to pray for me, when they hear
how far I am set apart from you by the burden of my
sins? If this is what they wish, I shall tell them what I am.
For no small good is gained, O Lord my God, if many
offer you thanks for me and many pray to you for me.
Let all who are truly my brothers love in me what they
know from your teaching to be worthy of their love,
and let them sorrow to find in me what they know from
your teaching to be occasion for remorse. This is what I
wish my true brothers to feel in their hearts. I do not
speak of strangers or of *alien foes, who make treacherous
promises, and lift their hands in perjury*. But my true
brothers are those who rejoice for me in their hearts
when they find good in me, and grieve for me when
they find sin. They are my true brothers, because
whether they see good in me or evil, they love me still.
To such as these I shall reveal what I am. Let them
breathe a sigh of joy for what is good in me and a sigh
of grief for what is bad. The good I do is done by you in
me and by your grace: the evil is my fault; it is the
punishment you send me. Let my brothers draw their

breath in joy for the one and sigh with grief for the other. Let hymns of thanksgiving and cries of sorrow rise together from their hearts, as though they were vessels burning with incense before you. And I pray you, O Lord, to be pleased with the incense that rises in your holy temple and, for your name's sake, to *have mercy on me, as you are ever rich in mercy*. Do not relinquish what you have begun, but make perfect what is still imperfect in me.

So, if I go on to confess, not what I was, but what I am, the good that comes of it is this. There is joy in my heart when I confess to you, yet there is fear as well; there is sorrow, and yet hope. But I confess not only to you but also to the believers among men, all who share my joy and all who, like me, are doomed to die; all who are my fellows in your kingdom and all who accompany me on this pilgrimage, whether they have gone before or are still to come or are with me as I make my way through life. They are your servants and my brothers. You have chosen them to be your sons. You have named them as the masters whom I am to serve if I wish to live with you and in your grace. This is your bidding, but it would hold less meaning for me if it were made known to me in words alone and I had not the example of Christ, who has shown me the way by his deeds as well. I do your bidding in word and deed alike. I do it beneath the protection of your wings, for the peril would be too great if it were not that my soul has submitted to you and sought the shelter of your wings and that my weakness is known to you. I am no more than a child, but my Father lives for ever and I have a Protector great enough to save me. For he who begot me and he who watches over me are one and the same, and for me there is no good but you, the Almighty, who are with me even before I am with you. So to such as you command me to serve I will reveal, not what I have been, but what I have become and what I am. But, since I do not *scrutinize my own conduct*, let my words be understood as they are meant.

30

It is truly your command that I should be continent and restrain myself from *gratification of corrupt nature, gratification of the eye, the empty pomp of living*. You commanded me not to commit fornication, and though you did not forbid me to marry, you counselled me to take a better course. You gave me the grace and I did your bidding, even before I became a minister of your sacrament. But in my memory, of which I have said much, the images of things imprinted upon it by my former habits still linger on. When I am awake they obtrude themselves upon me, though with little strength. But when I dream, they not only give me pleasure but are very much like acquiescence in the act. The power which these illusory images have over my soul and my body is so great that what is no more than a vision can influence me in sleep in a way that the reality cannot do when I am awake. Surely it cannot be that when I am asleep I am not myself, O Lord my God? And yet the moment when I pass from wakefulness to sleep, or return again from sleep to wakefulness, marks a great difference in me. During sleep where is my reason which, when I am awake, resists such suggestions and remains firm and undismayed even in face of the realities themselves? Is it sealed off when I close my eyes? Does it fall asleep with the senses of the body? And why is it that even in sleep I often resist the attractions of these images, for I remember my chaste resolutions and abide by them and give no consent to temptations of this sort? Yet the difference between waking and sleeping is so great that even when, during sleep, it happens otherwise, I return to a clear conscience when I wake and realize that, because of this difference, I was not responsible for the act, although I am sorry that by some means or other it happened to me.

The power of your hand, O God Almighty, is indeed great enough to cure all the diseases of my soul. By granting me more abundant grace you can even quench the fire of sensuality which provokes me in my sleep. More and more, O Lord, you will increase your gifts in me, so that my soul may follow me to you, freed from the concupiscence which binds it, and rebel no more against itself. By your grace it will no longer commit in sleep these shameful, unclean acts inspired by sensual images, which lead to the pollution of the body: it will not so much as consent to them. For to you, the Almighty, who are *powerful enough to carry out your purpose beyond all our hopes and dreams*, it is no great task to prescribe that no temptations of this kind, even such slight temptations as can be checked by the least act of will, should arouse pleasure in me, even in sleep, provided that my dispositions are chaste. This you can do for me at any time of life, even in the prime of manhood. But now I make this confession to my good Lord, declaring how I am still troubled by this kind of evil. *With awe in my heart I rejoice* in your gifts, yet I grieve for my deficiencies, trusting that you will perfect your mercies in me until I reach the fullness of peace, which I shall enjoy with you in soul and body, when *death is swallowed up in victory*.

35

I must now speak of a different kind of temptation, more dangerous than these because it is more complicated. For in addition to our bodily appetites, which make us long to gratify all our senses and our pleasures and lead to our ruin if we stay away from you by becoming their slaves, the mind is also subject to a certain propensity to use the sense of the body, not for self-indulgence of a physical kind, but for the satisfaction of its own inquisitiveness. This futile curiosity masquerades under the name of science and learning, and since it derives from our thirst for knowledge and sight is the principal sense by which knowledge is acquired, in the Scriptures it is called *gratification of the eye*. For although, correctly speaking, to see is the proper function of the eyes, we use the word of the other senses too, when we employ them to acquire knowledge. We do not say 'Hear how it glows', 'Smell how bright it is', 'Taste how it shines', or 'Feel how it glitters', because these are all things which we say that we see. Yet we not only say 'See how it shines' when we are speaking of something which only the eyes can perceive, but we also say 'See how loud it is', 'See how it smells', 'See how it tastes', and 'See how hard it is'. So, as I said, sense-experience in general is called the lust of the eyes because, although the function of sight belongs primarily to the eyes, we apply it to the other organs of sense as well, by analogy, when they are used to discover any item of knowledge.

We can easily distinguish between the motives of pleasure and curiosity. When the senses demand pleasure, they look for objects of visual beauty, harmonious sounds, fragrant perfumes, and things that are pleasant to the taste or soft to the touch. But when their motive is curiosity, they may look for just the reverse of these things, simply to put it to the proof, not for the sake of an unpleasant experience, but from a relish for investigation and discovery. What pleasure can there be in the sight of a mangled corpse, which can only horrify? Yet people will flock to see one lying on the ground, simply for the sensation of sorrow and horror that it gives them. They are even afraid that it may bring them nightmares, as though it were something that they had been forced to look at while they were awake or something to which they had been attracted by rumours of its beauty. The same is true of the other senses, although it would be tedious to give further examples. It is to satisfy this unhealthy curiosity that freaks and prodigies are put on show in the theatre, and for the same reason men are led to investigate the secrets of nature, which are irrelevant to our lives, although such knowledge is of no value to them and they wish to gain it merely for the sake of knowing. It is curiosity, too, which causes men to turn to sorcery in the effort to obtain knowledge for the same perverted purpose. And it even invades our religion, for we put God to the test when we demand signs and wonders from him, not in the hope of salvation, but simply for the love of the experience.

[. . .]

My life is full of such faults, and my only hope is in your boundless mercy. For when our hearts become repositories piled high with such worthless stock as this, it is the cause of interruption and distraction from our prayers. And although, in your presence, the voices of our hearts are raised to your ear, all kinds of trivial thoughts break in and cut us off from the great act of prayer.

41

I have now considered the sorry state to which my sins have brought me, according to the three different forms which temptation may take, and I have invoked your helping hand to save me. For in my wounded heart I saw your splendour and it dazzled me. I asked: Who can come close to such glory? *Your watchful care has lost sight of me.* You are the Truth which presides over all things. But in my selfish longing I did not wish to lose you. Together with you I wanted to possess a lie, much as a man will not utter so glaring a falsehood that it blinds his own eyes to the truth. And in this way I lost you, because you do not deign to be possessed together with a lie.

42

Whom could I find to reconcile me to you? Ought I to have sought the help of the angels? But if I had sought their help, what prayers should I have uttered? What rites should I have used? Many men, so I have heard, for lack of strength to return to you by themselves, have tried to do so by this means, but they ended by craving for strange visions, and their only reward was delusion. For they tried to find you in all the conceit and arrogance of their learning. They thrust out their chests in pride, when they should have beaten their breasts in mourning. And because they resembled them at heart, they attracted to their side the fallen angels, *the princes of the lower air*, their companions and associates in pride. But these allies tricked them, using magic craft, for while they sought a mediator who would cleanse them of their impurities, it was no mediator that they found. It was the devil, *passing for an angel of light*, and it was a potent lure for their proud flesh that he was not a creature of flesh and blood. For they were mortal men and sinners; but you, O Lord, to whom they wanted to be reconciled, are immortal and without sin. But a mediator between God and man must have something in common with God and something in common with man. For if in both these points he were like men, he would be far from God; and if in both of them he were like God, he would be far from men. In neither case could he be a mediator. But since, by the hidden pronouncements of your justice, you have given the devil licence to make a mockery of pride, he poses as a mediator. For in one point he is like man: he is sinful. And in the other he pretends to be like God: because he is not clothed with a mortal body of flesh and blood, he tries to represent himself as immortal. But since *sin offers death for wages*, in common with men he has this reason to be condemned to die.

43

But there is a true Mediator, whom in your secret mercy you have shown to men. You sent him so that by his example they too might learn humility. He is *the Mediator between God and men, Jesus Christ, who is a man,* and he appeared on earth between men, who are sinful and mortal, and God, who is immortal and just. Like men he was mortal: like God, he was just. And because the reward of the just is life and peace, he came so that by his own justness, which is his in union with God, he might make null the death of the wicked whom he justified, by choosing to share their death. He was made known to holy men in ancient times, so that they might be saved through faith in his passion to come, just as we are saved through faith in the passion he suffered long ago. For as man, he is our Mediator; but as the Word of God, he is not an intermediary between God and man because he is equal with God, and God with God, and together with him one God.

[...]

Terrified by my sins and the dead weight of my misery, I had turned my problems over in my mind and was half determined to seek refuge in the desert. But you forbade me to do this and gave me strength by saying: *Christ died for us all, so that being alive should no longer mean living with our own life, but with his life who died for us.* Lord, I cast all my troubles on you and from now on *I shall contemplate the wonders of your law.* You know how weak I am and how inadequate is my knowledge: teach me and heal my frailty. Your only Son, *in whom the whole treasury of wisdom and knowledge is stored up,* has redeemed me with his blood. *Save me from the scorn of my enemies,* for the price of my redemption is always in my thoughts. I eat it and drink it and minister it to others; and as one of the poor I long to be filled with it, to be one of those who *eat and have their fill.* And *those who look for the Lord will cry out in praise of him.*

Book XI

3

Let me hear and understand the meaning of the words: In the Beginning you made heaven and earth. Moses wrote these words. He wrote them and passed on into your presence, leaving this world where you spoke to him. He is no longer here and I cannot see him face to face. But if he were here, I would lay hold of him and in your name I would beg and beseech him to explain those words to me. I would be all ears to catch the sounds that fell from his lips. If he spoke in Hebrew, his words would strike my ear in vain and none of their meaning would reach my mind. If he spoke in Latin, I should know what he said. But how should I know whether what he said was true? If I knew this too, it could not be from him that I got such knowledge. But deep inside me, in my most intimate thought, Truth, which is neither Hebrew nor Greek nor Latin nor any foreign speech, would speak to me, though not in syllables formed by lips and tongue. It would whisper, 'He speaks the truth.' And at once I should be assured. In all confidence I would say to this man, your servant, 'What you tell me is true.'

Since, then, I cannot question Moses, whose words were true because you, the Truth, filled him with yourself, I beseech you, my God, to forgive my sins and grant me the grace to understand those words, as you granted him, your servant, the grace to speak them.

9

He is the Beginning, O God, in which you made heaven and earth. In this wonderful way you spoke and created them in your Word, in your Son, who is your Strength, your Wisdom, and your Truth.

Who can understand this mystery or explain it to others? What is that light whose gentle beams now and again strike through to my heart, causing me to shudder in awe yet firing me with their warmth? I shudder to feel how different I am from it: yet in so far as I am like it, I am aglow with its fire. It is the light of Wisdom, Wisdom itself, which at times shines upon me, parting my clouds. But when I weakly fall away from its light, those clouds envelop me again in the dense mantle of darkness which I bear for my punishment. For *my strength ebbs away for very misery,* so that I cannot sustain my blessings. And so I shall remain until you, O Lord, who *have pardoned all my sins,* also *heal all my mortal ills.* For you will *rescue my life from deadly peril, crown me with the blessings of your mercy, content all my desire for good, restore my youth as the eagle's plumage is restored. Our salvation is founded upon the hope of something,* and in endurance we await the fulfilment of your promises. Let those who are able listen to your voice speaking to their hearts. Trusting in your inspired words, I shall cry out: *What diversity, Lord, in your creatures! What wisdom has designed them all!* The

Beginning is Wisdom and Wisdom is the Beginning in which you made heaven and earth.

13

A fickle-minded man, whose thoughts were all astray because of his conception of time past, might wonder why you, who are God almighty, Creator of all, Sustainer of all, and Maker of heaven and earth, should have been idle and allowed countless ages to elapse before you finally undertook the vast work of creation. My advice to such people is to shake off their dreams and think carefully, because their wonder is based on a misconception.

How could those countless ages have elapsed when you, the Creator, in whom all ages have their origin, had not yet created them? What time could there have been that was not created by you? How could time elapse if it never was?

You are the Maker of all time. If, then, there was any time before you made heaven and earth, how can anyone say that you were idle? You must have made that time, for time could not elapse before you made it.

[. . .]

14

It is therefore true to say that when you had not made anything, there was no time, because time itself was of your making. And no time is co-eternal with you, because you never change; whereas, if time never changed, it would not be time.

[. . .]

19

In what way, then, do you, Ruler of all that you have created, reveal the future to the souls of men? You have revealed it to your prophets. But how do you reveal the future to us when, for us, the future does not exist? Is it that you only reveal present signs of things that are to come? For it is utterly impossible that things which do not exist should be revealed. The means by which you do this is far beyond our understanding. I have not the strength to comprehend this mystery, and by my own power I never shall. But in your strength I shall understand it, when you grant me the grace to see, sweet Light of the eyes of my soul.

[. . .]

25

I confess to you, Lord, that I still do not know what time is. Yet I confess too that I do know that I am saying this in time, that I have been talking about time for a long time, and that this long time would not be a long time if it were not for the fact that time has been passing all the while. How can I know this, when I do not know what time is? Is it that I do know what time is, but do not know how to put what I know into words? I am in a sorry state, for I do not even know what I do not know!

[...]

31

O Lord my God, how deep are your mysteries! How far from your safe haven have I been cast away by the consequences of my sins! Heal my eyes and let me rejoice in your light. If there were a mind endowed with such great power of knowing and foreknowing that all the past and all the future were known to it as clearly as I know a familiar psalm, that mind would be wonderful beyond belief. We should hold back from it in awe at the thought that nothing in all the history of the past and nothing in all the ages yet to come was hidden from it. It would know all this as surely as, when I sing the psalm, I know what I have already sung and what I have still to sing, how far I am from the beginning and how far from the end. But it is unthinkable that you, Creator of the universe, Creator of souls and bodies, should know all the past and all the future merely in this way. Your knowledge is far more wonderful, far more mysterious than this. It is not like the knowledge of a man who sings words well known to him or listens to another singing a familiar psalm. While he does this, his feelings vary and his senses are divided, because he is partly anticipating words still to come and partly remembering words already sung. It is far otherwise with you, for you are eternally without change, the truly eternal Creator of minds. In the Beginning you knew heaven and earth, and there was no change in your knowledge. In just the same way, in the Beginning you created heaven and earth, and there was no change in your action. Some understand this and some do not: let all alike praise you. You are supreme above all, yet your dwelling is in the humble of heart. For *you comfort the burdened*, and none fall who lift their eyes to your high place.

Book XII

2

Humbly my tongue confesses to you in the height of
your majesty that it was you who made heaven and
earth, the heaven I see and the earth I tread, from which,
too, came this earthly body that I bear. It was you
who made them. But where, O Lord, is the Heaven of
Heavens, of which we hear in the words of the psalm:
*To the Lord belongs the Heaven of Heavens, the earth he gives
to the children of men?* Where is that other heaven which
we cannot see and compared with which all that we see
is merely earth?

[. . .]

3

Undoubtedly the reason why we are told that this earth
was 'invisible and without form', a kind of deep abyss
over which there was no light, is that it had no form
whatsoever; and the reason why you commanded it to
be written that 'darkness reigned over the deep' could
only be that there was total absence of light. For if there
had been light, where else would it have been but high

above, shedding brilliance over all? But since as yet there was no light, what else was the presence of darkness but the absence of light? Darkness, then, reigned over all, because there was no light above, just as silence reigns where there is no sound. For what else is the presence of silence but the absence of sound?

[. . .]

4

How, then, could it be described in such a way that even dull minds could grasp it, except by means of some familiar word? And of all that goes to make up this world what can be found nearer to utter formlessness than 'earth' and 'the deep'? Since they are the lowest in the scale of created things, they have beauty of form in a lower degree than the other, higher things, which are radiant in their splendour. Why, then, should I not assume that the words 'earth, invisible and without form' are meant to convey to men, in a way that they can understand, that formless matter which you created without beauty in order to make from it this beautiful world?

7

If it was to be there first, in order to be the vehicle for all these visible, composite forms, what can have been its own origin? It can only have derived its being from you, for all things have their origin in you, whatever the degree of their being, although the less they are like you, the farther they are from you – and here I am not speaking in terms of space. This means, then, that you, O Lord, whose being does not alter as times change but is ever and always one and the same, the very same, *holy, holy, holy, Lord God Almighty*, made something in the Beginning, which is of yourself, in your Wisdom, which is born of your own substance, and you created this thing out of nothing.

You created heaven and earth but you did not make them of your own substance. If you had done so, they would have been equal to your only-begotten Son, and therefore to yourself, and justice could in no way admit that what was not of your own substance should be equal to you. But besides yourself, O God, who are Trinity in Unity, Unity in Trinity, there was nothing from which you could make heaven and earth. Therefore you must have created them from nothing, the one great, the other small. For there is nothing that you cannot do. You are good and all that you make must be good, both the great Heaven of Heavens and this little earth. You were, and besides you nothing was. From nothing, then, you created heaven and earth, distinct from one another; the one close to yourself, the other close to being nothing; the one surpassed only by yourself, the other little more than nothing.

13

This then, my God, is how I interpret your Scripture when I read the words: 'In the Beginning God made heaven and earth. The earth was invisible and without form, and darkness reigned over the deep.' Scripture does not say on which day you made them, and I understand the reason for this to be that 'heaven' here means the Heaven of Heavens – that is, the intellectual heaven, where the intellect is privileged to know all at once, not in part only, not as if it were *looking at a confused reflection in a mirror*, but as a whole, clearly, *face to face*; not first one thing and then another but, as I have said, all at once, quite apart from the ebb and flow of time – and 'earth' means the invisible, formless earth, also unaffected by the ebb and flow of time which always marks the change from this to that, since where there is no form there can be no this and no that. These, then, are the heaven and earth that are meant, as I understand it, when the Scripture says 'In the Beginning God made heaven and earth' without mention of day – heaven, that is, the Heaven of Heavens which was given form from the very beginning, and earth, that is, earth invisible and without order, which was utterly formless. In fact the Scripture explains in the very next sentence what earth is meant by this. And since it says that on the second day the firmament was made and that it was called heaven, it gives us to understand which heaven was meant by the first sentence, which makes no mention of days.

27

The account left by Moses, whom you chose to pass it on to us, is like a spring which is all the more copious because it flows in a confined space. Its waters are carried by a maze of channels over a wider area than could be reached by any single stream drawing its water from the same source and flowing through many different places. In the same way, from the words of Moses, uttered in all brevity but destined to serve a host of preachers, there gush clear streams of truth from which each of us, though in more prolix and roundabout phrases, may derive a true explanation of the creation as best he is able, some choosing one and some another interpretation.

[. . .]

31

For this reason, although I hear people say 'Moses meant this' or 'Moses meant that', I think it more truly religious to say 'Why should he not have had both meanings in mind, if both are true? And if others see in the same words a third, or a fourth, or any number of true meanings, why should we not believe that Moses saw them all? There is only one God, who caused Moses to write the Holy Scriptures in the way best suited to the minds of great numbers of men who would all see truths in them, though not the same truths in each case.'

For my part I declare resolutely and with all my heart that if I were called upon to write a book which was to be vested with the highest authority, I should prefer to write it in such a way that a reader could find re-echoed in my words whatever truths he was able to apprehend. I would rather write in this way than impose a single true meaning so explicitly that it would exclude all others, even though they contained no falsehood that could give me offence. And if this is what I would choose for myself, I will not be so rash, my God, as to suppose that so great a man as Moses deserved a lesser gift from you. As he wrote those words, he was aware of all that they implied. He was conscious of every truth that we can deduce from them and of others besides that we cannot, or cannot yet, find in them but are nevertheless there to be found.

32

[. . .]

O Lord my God, how much I have written on so few words! What endurance I should need and how much time, if I were to comment upon the whole of your Scriptures at such length! Let me, then, continue to lay before you my thoughts upon the Scriptures, but more briefly; and in so doing let me be content to give one explanation only, the one which I see by your inspiration to be true and certain and good, even though many may occur to me in places where more than one is possible.

Let me lay this confession before you in the firm belief that if the explanation I give accords with the meaning which Moses had in mind, I shall have done what is right and best. This is what I must try my utmost to do. But if I fail, let me at least say what your Truth wills to reveal to me by the words of Scripture, just as he revealed what he willed to Moses.

Book XIII

1

I call upon you, O God, my Mercy, who made me and did not forget me when I forgot you. I call you to come into my soul, for by inspiring it to long for you you prepare it to receive you. Now, as I call upon you, do not desert me, for you came to my aid even before I called upon you. In all sorts of ways, over and over again, when I was far from you, you coaxed me to listen to your voice, to turn my back on you no more, and to call upon you for aid when, all the time, you were calling to me yourself. You blotted out all my evil deeds, in order not to repay me with the punishment I deserved for the work of my hands, which had led me away from you; and even before I did them, you took into account all the good deeds by which I should deserve well of you, in order to recompense yourself for the work of your hands which made me. For before I was, you were: I was nothing, that you should give me being. Yet now I am; and this is because out of your goodness you provided for all that you have made me and all from which you have made me. You had no need of me, nor am I a creature good in such a way as to be helpful to you, my Lord and my God. It is not as though you could grow tired by working and I could serve you by preventing your fatigue, nor would your power be any the less if my service were lacking. I cannot serve you as a peasant tills the land, for your works bear fruit even if I fail to serve you with my husbandry. I can only serve you and worship you so that good may come to me from you, and but for you no good could come to me, for I should not even exist to receive it.

3

At the beginning of creation you said *Let there be light; and the light began.* I think these words are properly to be understood to refer to the spiritual creation, because it was already life of a certain kind, able to be given light by you. But just as, previously, it could make no claim on you, by its own deserts, to be the kind of life which could receive your light, so, now that it existed, it could not claim to receive this gift by its own merits. In its formless state it would not have been pleasing to you unless it became light. And it became light, not simply by existing, but by fixing its gaze upon you and clinging to you, the Light which shone upon it. In this way it owes to your grace, and to your grace alone, both the gift of its very existence and the gift of a life that is lived in happiness. For, by undergoing a change, which bettered it, it was turned towards that which cannot change, either for better or for worse, that is, towards you. Only you can never change, because you alone are absolute simplicity, for whom to live is the same as to live in blessed happiness, since you are your own beatitude.

5

When I read that your Spirit moved over the waters, I
catch a faint glimpse of the Trinity which you are, my
God. For it was you, the Father, who created heaven
and earth in the Beginning of our Wisdom – which is
your Wisdom, born of you, equal to you, and co-eternal
with you – that is, in your Son. I have had much to say
of the Heaven of Heavens, of the earth invisible and
without form, and of the deep, showing how its darkness
was in keeping with the spiritual creation, which, in its
formlessness, had no cohesion or stability. Such it would
have remained unless, by being turned to God, from
whom it already drew such life as it had, it had received
beauty as well as life by the reflection of his glory. In this
way the Heaven of Heavens came into being, that is, the
heaven of the heaven which was later created between
the waters above and the waters below. When I spoke
of these things, I took the word 'God', who made them,
to mean the Father and the 'Beginning', in which he
made them, to mean the Son. But, believing that my
God is a Trinity, I searched for this truth in the sacred
words of his Scripture and found it where it says that
your Spirit moved over the waters. Here, then, is the
Trinity, my God, Father, Son, and Holy Ghost, the
Creator of all creation.

11

Who can understand the omnipotent Trinity? We all speak of it, though we may not speak of it as it truly is, for rarely does a soul know what it is saying when it speaks of the Trinity. Men wrangle and dispute about it, but it is a vision that is given to none unless they are at peace.

There are three things, all found in man himself, which I should like men to consider. They are far different from the Trinity, but I suggest them as a subject for mental exercise by which we can test ourselves and realize how great this difference is. The three things are existence, knowledge, and will, for I can say that I am, I know, and I will. I am a being which knows and wills; I know both that I am and that I will; and I will both to be and to know. In these three – being, knowledge, and will – there is one inseparable life, one life, one mind, one essence; and therefore, although they are distinct from one another, the distinction does not separate them. This must be plain to anyone who has the ability to understand it. In fact he need not look beyond himself. Let him examine himself closely, take stock, and tell me what he finds.

But when he has found a common principle in these three and has told me what he finds, he must not think that he has discovered that which is above them all and is unchangeable, that which immutably is, immutably knows, and immutably wills. For none of us can easily conceive whether God is a Trinity because all these three – immutable being, immutable knowledge, and immutable will – are together in him; whether all three are together in each person of the Trinity, so that each is threefold; or whether both these suppositions are true and in some wonderful way, in which the simple and the multiple are one, though God is infinite he is yet an end to himself and in himself, so that the Trinity is in itself, and is known to itself, and suffices to itself, the supreme Being, one alone immutably, in the vastness of its unity. This is a mystery that none can explain, and which of us would presume to assert that he can?

28

And you saw all that you had made, O God, and found it very good. We, too, see all these things and know that they are very good. In the case of each of your works you first commanded them to be made, and when they had been made you looked at each in turn and saw that it was good. I have counted and found that Scripture tells us seven times that you saw that what you had made was good, and when you looked for the eighth time and saw the whole of your creation, we are told that you found it not only good but very good, for you saw all at once as one whole. Each separate work was good, but when they were all seen as one, they were not merely good: they were very good.

The same can be said of every material thing which has beauty. For a thing which consists of several parts, each beautiful in itself, is far more beautiful than the individual parts which, properly combined and arranged, compose the whole, even though each part, taken separately, is itself a thing of beauty.

35

O Lord God, grant us peace, for all that we have is your gift. Grant us the peace of repose, the peace of the Sabbath, the peace which has no evening. For this worldly order in all its beauty will pass away. All these things that are very good will come to an end when the limit of their existence is reached. They have been allotted their morning and their evening.

37

In that eternal Sabbath you will rest in us, just as now you work in us. The rest that we shall enjoy will be yours, just as the work that we now do is your work done through us. But you, O Lord, are eternally at work and eternally at rest. It is not in time that you see or in time that you move or in time that you rest: yet you make what we see in time; you make time itself and the repose which comes when time ceases.

38

We see the things which you have made, because they exist. But they only exist because you see them. Outside ourselves we see that they exist, and in our inner selves we see that they are good. But when you saw that it was right that they should be made, in the same act you saw them made.

It was only after a lapse of time that we were impelled to do good, that is, after our hearts had received the inspiration of the Holy Spirit, Before then our impulse was to do wrong, because we had deserted you. But you, who are the one God, the good God, have never ceased to do good. By the gift of your grace some of the works that we do are good, but they are not everlasting. After them we hope that we shall find rest, when you admit us to the great holiness of your presence. But you are Goodness itself and need no good besides yourself. You are for ever at rest, because you are your own repose.

What man can teach another to understand this truth? What angel can teach it to an angel? What angel can teach it to a man? We must ask it of you, seek it in you; we must knock at your door. Only then shall we receive what we ask and find what we seek; only then will the door be opened to us.